Trade Your Way to Wealth

Founded in 1807, John Wiley & Sons is the oldest independent publishing company in the United States. With offices in North America, Europe, Australia, and Asia, Wiley is globally committed to developing and marketing print and electronic products and services for our customers' professional and personal knowledge and understanding.

The Wiley Trading series features books by traders who have survived the market's ever changing temperament and have prospered—some by reinventing systems, others by getting back to basics. Whether a novice trader, professional, or somewhere in between, these books will provide the advice and strategies needed to prosper today and well into the future.

For a list of available titles, visit our web site at www.WileyFinance.com.

Trade Your Way to Wealth

Earn Big Profits with No-Risk, Low-Risk, and Measured-Risk Strategies

BILL KRAFT

John Wiley & Sons, Inc.

Published by John Wiley & Sons, Inc., Hoboken, New Jersey.
Published simultaneously in Canada.

For general information on our other products and services or for technical support, please contact our Customer Care Department within the United States at (800) 762-2974, outside the United States at (317) 572-3993 or fax (317) 572-4002.

Wiley also publishes its books in a variety of electronic formats. Some content that appears in print may not be available in electronic formats. For more information about Wiley products, visit our Web site at www.wiley.com.

Charts produced by Telechart2005® which is a registered trademark of Worden Brothers, Inc., Five Oaks Office Park, 4905 Pine Cone Drive, Durham, NC 27707. Ph (800) 776-4940 or (919) 408-0542.

Library of Congress Cataloging-in-Publication Data:

Kraft, Bill, 1943-
    Trade your way to wealth : earn big profits with no-risk, low-risk, and measured-risk strategies / Bill Kraft.
        p. cm.—(Wiley trading series)
    Includes index.
    ISBN 978-0-470-12979-1 (cloth)
    1. Investments.   2. Stocks.   3. Options (Finance)   4. Exchange traded funds.   I. Title.
        HG4521.K687 2008
        332.63'22—dc22

                                                                                2007020338

Printed in the United States of America.

10 9 8 7 6 5 4 3 2 1

This book is dedicated to those who want to improve their financial lot in life and who are willing to make the effort necessary to accomplish that goal.

Contents

Preface

We live in a time when we have no choice but to take care of ourselves. We can no longer count on high-paying jobs, pensions, and government entitlement programs to assure our financial health. We must do it ourselves. I know many people who *want* to increase their net worth but are so afraid of losing that they do nothing.

I have written this book to show you how to trade fearlessly, without worry. You'll be able to sleep soundly at night knowing you have little or no risk, or at least that you are only taking risks with which you are comfortable. You will see how to remove risk while finding ways to make great returns.

WHY TRADE

I love to trade. It is my passion for many reasons. I have the ability to trade anywhere in the world. As long as I can connect to the Internet, I can be trading. Nowadays that means almost everywhere. I wrote this preface on the island of Kauai, one of the most remote places on earth, and I just finished about an hour online, during which time I closed trades that realized over $10,000 in profits. In my view, that is really cool. Since the markets open around 4:30 AM and close around 1:00 PM Hawaiian time, I have the remainder of the day to do whatever I please. My stops are in place so my account can run on "autopilot." My commute is about 20 or 30 steps, just as it is at home. I have no boss, no employees, and no mounds of paper requiring my daily attention. I set my own hours and I have plenty of time to devote to my family. I do not have to worry about someone at work backstabbing me or trying to take my job. All I need is a broker, a computer, and a charting service, and I am in business. Even if there is no electricity, I could use a solar-powered computer like the one on the forbidden island of Ni'ihau. I am able to give to my chosen charities. Above all, I make enough money to enjoy a fantastic quality of life. Why wouldn't I love trading?

I am continually amazed by the vast majority who toil so long and so hard at their employment just working to make ends meet. I have talked to many who struggle from paycheck to paycheck, believing that working for someone else is their security, but wondering if they will ever be able to retire. The excuses to avoid investing are legion. I do not have the time, most say. The truth is that almost anyone can take time to learn to invest and to learn to invest in low-risk or even no-risk ways. If they would only make that time, they might find that they have more time than they ever imagined, as well as enough money to do the things they truly enjoy.

WHAT THIS BOOK COVERS

This book is designed to help anyone—from novice to experienced investor—improve their quality of life and generate increased wealth. It begins with the pros and cons of "buy and hold" investing, which, by the way, is not for everyone. From there, I show you, in step-by-step fashion, how to create your own personal business plan. Successful investors always tell you to have a plan, but this book will show you what your plan should include and how to create it.

With this plan in place, I will then show you a variety of great money-making strategies from *zero* risk to pretty risky. Unlike so many other books, I try to show you where the risks exist and ways to deal with many of them so that you can invest in a comfort zone.

I examine many strategies that explode the myth that option trading is always risky. The fact is that many times option trading has significantly less risk than buying a stock. You will learn how to make money when the market is going up, when the market is going down, and even when it is going sideways. I will even show you how to "insure" your stock positions.

Exchange-traded funds (ETFs) are becoming more and more popular, so we will see why they can be wonderful investment tools and explore when and how to use them to your greatest advantage. We will also see how they should be chosen, when positions should be entered, and what ETFs to avoid.

Since almost everyone needs income, I will show you ways in which to invest in low-risk, high-yield vehicles that you can trade like a stock. Many of the examples will actually be free of federal tax, and I will show you examples where the income can be double tax free—free of both federal and state taxes.

NOW YOU CAN CREATE YOUR OWN ROAD MAP TO FINANCIAL SUCCESS

When you have finished this book, it is my fervent hope and sincere belief that you will be able to use the information to invest in a manner that is comfortable for you. You will have learned many ways to make a lot of money, vastly improve your quality of life, and still remain in your comfort zone. You will be able to create your own path to greater financial success. In short, you will be able to trade wisely and fearlessly.

Bill Kraft
Kauai, HI

Acknowledgments

I do not want to sound like a speech at the Oscars, but I do have many people to thank. Most of all, thanks to my wonderful wife, Patti, who helped and encouraged me all the way and without whose support this project would have been much more difficult. I also want to acknowledge my grown children, Billy and Laurie, and their families for adding the joy to my life that makes each day precious. Thanks to the many teachers who led me to this point in my life.

Thanks, also, to Kevin Commins at John Wiley & Sons, who sought me out to write this book, and to my fantastic editor, Emilie Herman, whose gentle guidance helped ease me through the process of writing this book.

Finally, I thank Worden Brothers, Inc. and their Director of Business & Client Relations, Michael Thompson, for permitting me to use copies of their wonderful charts in this book.

C.W.K. III

Trade Your Way to Wealth

CHAPTER 1

Millions Can Be Made with Safer Trades

There are a number of ways to trade the stock and options markets without fear. In this book, I am going to show you some strategies that can yield exceptional returns with little or sometimes even *no* risk. Whether you are a market neophyte or someone who has been investing for years, you need to know how to protect yourself and make money at the same time. I want you to see some of the strategies I have used to increase my own wealth and, at the same time, permit me to sleep soundly at night.

Fear is one of the great enemies to profitable trading. Fear results from risk taking. If we can remove some or all of the risk from our trading equation, we will become better traders and investors. This book is designed to do exactly that—show you how to reduce and even remove risk from your trades and investments.

Many of us in the Baby Boomer generation were taught that if we went to work for a corporation and were loyal to that company, we would be set for life. We would have a pension to carry us through our older years. On top of that, we would enjoy the benefits of Social Security. As so many workers have learned, security can be illusory. Some companies have underfunded pensions, other companies have disappeared, and still others have laid off or fired workers before pension rights vested.

Politics aside, there is little doubt that Social Security as originally envisioned is a failure. Without dramatic change, it is headed for bankruptcy. For those who have relied on the promise of corporate pensions and Social Security benefits, the future could be grim unless they can develop an investment plan that will take the place of the income streams they thought they were going to enjoy.

Those just entering their productive years will need to look forward. They will need to educate their children, buy their homes, cover their living expenses, and pay for their medical care. It seems highly unlikely that they will be able to count on future pensions or Social Security. In fact, as things stand now, more of their earnings will be taken to fund the preceding generations' needs. If you are in this group that is just entering their earnings years, you, too, will need to have an investment plan that will enable you to achieve the lifestyle you desire.

As we go forward, you'll see some ways to help make your money grow, help you achieve financial goals, and help enhance the quality of your life. Please don't think these things will happen automatically. This isn't a get-rich-quick scheme; I'm looking at ways to try to increase wealth while keeping risk to a minimum.

Success in these endeavors requires some study as well as a plan. I'll give you a simple framework so you can develop a personal plan that fits you and your personal situation. I'll also lead you through some strategies that I know can be successful. It'll be up to you to study them, test them, practice them, and decide what you want to do. Nothing here will be very complicated, and I'll try to take you through step by step. You'll see that you can set up no-risk and low-risk trades yourself.

Learning the same things I am going to show you in this book changed my life, and it can change yours as well.

HOW I CHANGED CAREERS AND LEARNED HOW TO TRADE FOR A LIVING

Ten years ago, I knew almost nothing about successful trading and investing. I had practiced law for 25 years. My law practice had been successful, but it wasn't much fun. In the last several years of practice, my primary client was a major corporation and my actions were controlled, second-guessed, and subjected to the vagaries of corporate politics. I felt nothing but relief when the client ended our relationship, and I decided it was time to do something I really enjoyed for a change—so I opened a photography store. Photography had been a passion for some time, and I thought a photo processing store and portrait studio would be just the ticket.

I quickly learned that the business had little to do with my passion and that I was tied to a retail operation. I was working 7 days a week, at least 10 hours a day, and the biggest paycheck I took home was around $200. Photographic processing equipment was very expensive, and most of my assets were tied up in the business. I was trying to make a success of the store, but the business was turning digital and things were getting worse.

Things seemed as bad as they could get, but then I suffered a great personal tragedy. As a result of that loss, I decided to get rid of the store and find something else to do. I definitely did not want to return to the practice of law, so I began my search. I explored and tried many different things, including a stint selling preneed funerals. Nothing was clicking.

One morning, in an airport, I bought a book to read on a plane ride back east. The book was about trading. I read it on the flight, and I reread it five times. I knew I had found my new vocation. I was going to become a stock and option trader. Shortly after I had read the book, I received a flyer in the mail advertising a free seminar that the same author was giving near where I lived. My bride and I knew that the free seminar would be a "come-on" for some expensive seminar, so we agreed that we would go to the free seminar and see what we could pick up. We also agreed that the seminar that was being sold would probably be too expensive so we wouldn't sign up for it.

Well, we went to the free seminar and we were sold. We bought the seminar that we thought would be too expensive. Remember, now, I was almost out of money. We flew to the West Coast and attended the seminar for two days. It ended on a Friday, and by the following Tuesday, we had made back the cost of the seminar using the trading knowledge we had just gained.

That seminar was in the early fall, and the same company was having another seminar in Hawaii in November. We signed up for that seminar and, while in Hawaii, made about $26,000. If I hadn't been sold on trading before, I was then. I began my career as a full-time trader. Of course, what I didn't realize was that I was involved in what was perhaps the biggest bull market in U.S. history. It was hard to lose on a trade. Then came the year 2000, and the bubble burst. I had purchased one stock for around $88 a share and finally got rid of it at around $3. Fortunately, I owned only a few shares.

I learned several lessons from that experience. I learned that the belief that "it's coming back" isn't necessarily very wise; I learned that "buy and hold" can be a dangerous strategy; I learned that I better find out how to trade a down market; I learned that I needed to keep learning; and, most importantly, I learned that risk awareness and risk control are critically important to success.

I continued to study and continued to learn. I read everything about trading I could get my hands on and I attended many seminars. I was so excited about trading that I would bore almost everyone I met with conversations about trading. I did well. If people seemed interested in my stories about trading and my successes, I would invite them to the house to learn what I was doing. (As an aside, I should mention that one of the great benefits I consider I have from trading is that I can do it at home. In fact, I can do it wherever I can hook up my laptop.) Family, friends, and neighbors came to learn, and they came and they came. It got to the point where I had someone at home learning to trade for five or six hours every trading day so I ran out of time to trade myself.

I then had an "aha!" moment.

I decided I'd do seminars and if the students had to pay they wouldn't come. I did some radio advertising and set up some classes. I was wrong. They paid and they did come. Now I had another business and it was very successful. However, while seminars are fun for me to do, my real passion is trading. At most, I work only two or three hours a day trading, but setting up and running seminars is a full-time business. I decided to significantly reduce the numbers of seminars and made a DVD of the basic SWAT (Stockmarket Weapons and Tactics) seminar. I now give seminars only rarely and advertise infrequently. Most attendees find me by word of mouth.

As a result of the seminars, I was approached by a publisher to do some advisory services. My services differ from many in that I am not interested in sending out a "tip of the day" or a "tip of the week." In fact, I just send out some of the trades I am actually doing myself in an attempt to provide education to subscribers. I always try to include a technical explanation of what I am doing. I sincerely believe that it is a serious mistake for anyone to blindly follow someone else's trade. Each individual has a personal risk tolerance, a different set of investing or trading goals, different amounts of money to risk, different levels of knowledge and experience, and different approaches to life.

Instead of trying to follow what someone else does, I believe that anyone who wants to trade successfully must first learn about themselves, then about trading and investing, and finally about what trades suit them.

SUCCESS WORKING A COUPLE OF HOURS A DAY

Investing and trading has led to a wonderful life and lifestyle for my wife and me. I now work only a couple of hours a day trading. I have a great deal of time to devote to my family. My wife and I are able to travel frequently and widely. We are able to give time and money to charity and volunteer work. We are not tied to the daily regimen required by a normal job, and our financial future is secure. I have become a multimillionaire. We can travel whenever and wherever we choose, and I can set up shop anywhere I have access to the Internet.

This book is, in part, an effort to give back. It is an effort to show the reader ways that make it possible to enhance retirement, to heighten quality of life, and to attempt to assure a financially comfortable future. There are, of course, no guarantees. I can show you strategies that may yield great returns at known levels of risk, some even at *no risk*. I can show you where many of the risks lie and I can show you ways in which to reduce and minimize risk. The risks taken, however, will always be yours, so it is important to gain an understanding of not only how to make money but also to learn how to avoid losing money.

HOW TO CREATE A SUCCESSFUL TRADING PLAN AND SLEEP SOUNDLY AT THE SAME TIME

As we go forward, I'll set out the details of exactly how to set up a trading plan that can help you sleep soundly while letting your money work for you. Sound sleep is, in part, a product of knowing and limiting risk; it is a product of placing yourself in a position where the risk undertaken is one with which you are comfortable. In Chapter 3, we'll cover, in detail, just how to create that kind of plan. Ultimately, the plan will be your own and it will be one that puts you in a position where the level of risk undertaken is comfortable for you. Unless you can find a comfortable level of risk, you'll just find stress influencing your trading. Whenever stress or emotion enters the trading process, it is likely to be a serious negative.

It has often been said and written that fear and greed move the markets. While that statement is true, it is also true that traders who trade under stress and whose decisions are a product of fear or greed are those who are least likely to succeed. So let us remove the stress and learn to trade with as much discipline and as little emotion as possible.

THE ZERO-RISK TRADE MAY BE FOR YOU

Your personality may dictate that you take no financial risk at all. If that is the case, you will love the zero-risk trade. Even if you are a little more aggressive, the zero-risk trade is something you will probably want to add to your arsenal of investment strategies. Zero-risk trades do exist. They are frequently employed by the very wealthy whose first goal is to preserve capital. In the zero-risk trade, you can assure yourself that your capital will be safe and you'll see that a significant return is possible even where nothing is risked.

We'll also explore low-risk trades, where really high returns are possible with little risk. Only you can judge the risk you are willing to take, but we'll look at strategies and trades that will satisfy anyone from the most conservative trader to those willing to accept a bit more risk in return for even higher rewards.

HOW TO CUT LOSSES AND LET PROFITS RUN

One of the old adages about successful trading and investing is "cut your losses and let your profits run." Easily said and quite true, but rare is the person who knows how to do either, let alone both. Many traders, new and old alike, realize the wisdom of the saying, but have never learned what it actually means or how to cut losses and let profits run. The failure to cut losses or let profits run is usually the result of letting emotions rule the trade rather than trading in a disciplined, unemotional fashion.

As we go forward, I will try to show you some of the ways to eliminate emotions from trading and develop a disciplined method that can work for you.

CHAPTER 2

Is the Invest-and-Hold Strategy Best for You?

O f all the strategies used by the general trading public, buy-and-hold is probably the best known and most commonly utilized by far. My question is: hold until when? Death? That can be great for the heirs, but what about the investor during his lifetime?

My dad was a buy-and-hold investor who started investing in stock in the 1960s and held until he passed away in 2002. Fortunately, he didn't need the money and the strategy worked out very well, particularly for me and his other heirs. That isn't always the case, however.

All investors should carefully evaluate their goals, risk tolerance, needs, time frame, and available assets when deciding which strategy or strategies are appropriate for their individual circumstances. Chapter 3 will cover the creation of a specific plan in detail. For now, though, it is important to recognize that any given strategy may or may not be appropriate for a particular investor. Consideration must also be given to diversification beyond stock or option strategies and may include investments such as real estate, annuities, or even futures.

Each investor needs to decide whether all, part, or any of his portfolio should fall into the buy-and-hold category. On the plus side, history has shown that the markets have tended to go up over time. The Dow 30 Industrials, for example, rose from a low of about 760 in 1966 to over 11,800 forty years later in 2006. Over that same time, the S&P 500 climbed from around 74 to over 1,350. The Nasdaq moved from around 375 in 1990 to over 2,300 in 2006, but we must remember it reached as high as 5,000+ before plummeting in 2000.

Using the Dow (when I say Dow, I mean the Dow 30 Industrials) as an example, in order to enjoy the gains, one must have held all the components through the whole period, and some of those component stocks did change over time. That means that some of the stocks had to have been sold and replaced by others. In such instances, *hold* would have meant until the stock was no longer part of the Dow.

Nowadays, that is no longer a real issue because we can buy exchange-traded funds (ETFs) that track various indices like the Dow, Nasdaq, and S&P 500. I'll have a lot more to say about ETFs in Chapter 8, but for now, it is sufficient to know that we don't have to buy every stock in an index and sell and replace a stock each time it is removed from the index. Instead, we can trade the index using the appropriate ETF.

Suppose that we did buy all the components of an index, or at least an ETF that tracked an index. What if we needed cash at some specific point in time? A family certainly could face an expensive medical emergency or might need funds because of the loss of a job, or perhaps there could be a reason to buy a new home or the investor could come upon an enticing real estate investment or need to fund the cost of a wedding. There are a myriad of reasons why cash might be needed quickly and unexpectedly. Such events—emergency or otherwise—do occur in life, so the "hold until when" question may well be answered by influences completely outside the investor's control. That could be good or bad. Even though the markets have gone up over time, that doesn't mean that there haven't been periods where they have fallen off, retraced, been flat, or even crashed.

Take a look at Figure 2.1. Someone who bought the Nasdaq tracking ETF (symbol: QQQQ) near a low in the latter part of 1999 might have gotten

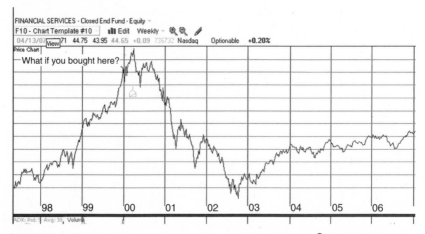

FIGURE 2.1 Price Movement of QQQQ. (Telechart 2005® chart courtesy of Worden Brothers, Inc.)

in around $61 a share. If circumstances forced them to get out in early 2000, they may have exited around $116. However, if they got in at the same time, but suffered an emergency toward the beginning of the last quarter of 2002, they may have suffered a devastating loss by getting out when QQQQ had dropped to the low 20s. In fact, even as of late 2006, they would not have gotten back to breakeven from the entry in 1999. The free-fall period from 2000 to 2002 would not have been the time to have been forced out of the market, particularly the Nasdaq.

Ownership of an individual stock can have an even more dramatic effect. Buying Microsoft (MSFT) in its early days and holding through its nine splits would have done wonders for any investor's net worth. Berkshire Hathaway's Class A shares (BRKA) that traded in the $100,000-*a-share* range in 2006 could have been purchased for a paltry $5,500 a share back in 1990. On the other hand, the horrors of buy and hold became evident to owners of Enron and WorldCom when the stocks collapsed and became worthless.

Employees of many companies have participated in various stock ownership programs over the years. Some have done very well and others have simply failed. Over the years, I have spoken to many people who have owned stock in the companies for which they worked, and one of the common traits I have observed is that these employees don't want to sell any of their company's stock even when they can. Sometimes their reluctance to sell is based on loyalty to the company; sometimes it is based on fear that there might be some retribution if they sell their shares. Though I have spoken to many people about writing covered calls on their stock (a subject with which I'll deal later and in some depth), they fear to do so.

Writing covered calls is a way to make monthly income on stock you own, but one of the possible consequences is that you may have to sell your stock at a profit. Even knowing that they can make money—sometimes serious money—every month on their company stock, these folks have feared to engage the strategy. They are buy-and-hold strategists, sometimes to their absolute and literal financial ruin.

One of my hopes in writing this book is to help people avoid such ruin. I want to show you ways to protect yourselves—ways to use your common sense to apply strategies that will advance the ball, not leave you in a position where you have to work until you're 75 or 80 or 85. In my estimation it is critically important not to buy and hold blindly or out of fear. In Chapter 3 we talk about creating your own personal plan, and one of the things I emphasize is a preplanned exit.

In my view, nothing in trading and investing is more important than an exit. As you will see, a good entry in a position is defined by where the initial exit will be. Entering a position without knowing where your exit will be in the event the play turns against you is a pretty sure way to the poorhouse. When you decide to buy and hold, I suggest you must define "hold 'til when." Hold 'til death may be your answer, but I can assure you that holding until death isn't the way to go for most investors.

SUMMARY

As you will soon see, successful trading can be quite simple. That doesn't mean it is easy. It requires the removal of emotion and replacing emotion with discipline. In trading, I don't believe discipline can exist without a plan, so the next thing we are going to do is look at how you can create a plan for yourself. Using your plan, you will be able to enter positions with predetermined risks, low risk, and even no risk.

In this chapter, I've tried to show you some of the risks of the buy-and-hold strategy. Little is riskier than simply buying an individual stock with the intent of doing nothing but holding it. Think of the bad things that can happen when you buy a stock and do nothing else to protect your position. The company can go bankrupt (like some airlines, for example), the CEO can be arrested and go to jail, the CFO can be caught with his hand in the cookie jar, a competitor can come up with a better product, the company's product can become obsolete (use that Victrola much anymore?), and even the stock of a great company may just go sideways or drift down.

I've raised all these negatives so you will appreciate investment risk to a greater degree than you have in the past. I intend to spend most of the rest of the book showing you ways to control, reduce, or eliminate risk in your portfolio or at least in parts of it. I hope you will come away armed with new knowledge and with new strategies that can keep you away from the dangerous ledges as you climb financial heights you only dreamed possible.

CHAPTER 3

Successful Trading Can Be Simple

M y experience has taught me that successful trading can be simple. That does not mean that it is necessarily easy. Success in trading, as in many other areas of life, has a few prerequisites. In trading, they include the development of a personal plan, careful management of money, discipline, and knowledge. Without all of those factors, the trader is unlikely to stay ahead in the long run. Luck can play an important role, but it is usually only a temporary one. In order to stay the course, luck is not enough. The "hunch bet" can undoubtedly pay off sometimes, but "betting it all on black" is not the best way to go over time. The successful trader is a businessperson, not a gambler.

Gambling does not strike me as a particularly good way to try to get through retirement or send the kids to college. If we can follow a trail that has little risk and potentially great rewards, I am sure we will be better off than the vast majority of those who risk it all.

The following sections include specific considerations that are designed to assist you in the creation of your personal road map to increased wealth.

HAVE A BUSINESS PLAN

A number of years ago, I was invited to New York to the offices of a large, high-powered brokerage firm. The invitation was extended because I had complained repeatedly to my local broker about their online trading site. In my view it was atrocious and of little use to anyone who did anything other than first buy stock and later sell it. It was worthless for trading options. The firm was quite proud of their site and really could not understand why I had such a low opinion of it. As an aside, I should mention that they listened politely to my suggestions and have ignored them to this day. In any event, I was invited onto their massive trading floor and introduced to their head trader.

What a wonderful opportunity for a relatively new trader like I was! I was able to spend about a half hour, one on one, with this brilliant trader. After answering my many questions, he asked me what I was doing in my own trading. I outlined my complete plan and strategy and waited for him to marvel at how clever I was. Instead, he said it was great that I had a plan. Any plan, he said, was better than none, and most of the retail traders he met had no plan. He went on to explain that he found that almost all traders he met who had no plan failed. However, he observed that those who did have a plan generally enjoyed at least some measure of success.

That lesson stuck with me. It may be the single most important thing I have learned over my many years of trading. In the trading seminars I teach, I always emphasize the importance of having a business plan. Trading, after all, is a business. What other business venture would we consider or enter without first having a plan?

When I began teaching seminars, I would simply tell the class that they each needed to have a plan. They would all nod dutifully and wait for me to get to "the good stuff." They wanted to hear how I made money. The fact is that the plan is the foundation of the way I make money in the markets. Just like students cannot learn algebra or calculus until they have learned basic math, a trader cannot be successful unless he or she has a basic foundation, and the first blocks of that foundation must be a plan.

As I said, in my earlier seminar classes, I taught the need for a plan. In the more advanced classes, I would ask students questions about their plan and I was invariably met with a "deer in the headlights" stare. I thought they were only interested in trying to get rich quickly and too lazy to work out their own plan. Then one day I asked a student why she had not created a plan and she said simply: "I don't know how." I realized that it was my failure as a teacher, not her failure as a student, that she (and many other students) had no plan.

Ever since that incident, I have included a simple sheet outlining some factors traders need to consider in formulating their own plan. I go over each element in class, and I'll go through them here in some detail so you can begin your plan in case you do not already have one. Once you have reviewed the detailed suggestions in the following sections, you can refer to Appendix A for a quick checklist of the elements I suggest you include in your plan.

ELEMENTS OF A TRADING PLAN

One thing that is important to realize about the business plan is that it will be created for your needs. You probably noticed that I have referred to the plan as "your plan" or "their own plan." I have used those phrases because the trading business plan is, indeed, your personal plan. It is not a plan for everyone; it is a plan for you and you alone. If we think about it, each of us is at a different point in life: we each have individual goals and different personalities; we are different ages; we have different tolerances for risk, different amounts of money to invest, different knowledge, different amounts of time we are willing or able to devote to our investing, different family situations, and so forth. You get the picture. You are unique, and so, too, will your plan be.

As you are about to see, some of the elements of your plan will be easily answered while others may require more thought and, perhaps, more knowledge. Hopefully, by the end of this book, you'll have a plan in place so you can follow the old adage "plan your trade and trade your plan." If you do, you will definitely be ahead of the crowd.

What follows are some of the questions you need to answer to create your own plan.

Will I Trade Full Time or Part Time?

This question is usually pretty easy to answer. Most people are employed, so full-time trading is not yet something they can do. It cannot be part of their plan right away. Of course, longer term, they may well find that they enjoy trading and that it is so lucrative that they do intend to do it full time—eventually. In my own case, I had already left my law practice and sold my photo studio (for very little, by the way) when I was drawn to trading. I began as a full-time trader and it became my passion. Failure was not an option.

How Much Risk Money Will I Assign to My Investing Business?

This question might be a little more difficult to answer. It requires some thought about the definition of *risk money*. In the seminars, I define risk money as money one can afford to lose. In other words, it is money that is not needed for necessities like groceries, rent, mortgage payments, car payments, insurance premiums, tuition, or the like. Of course, all money invested is not necessarily at risk. Later on, for example, we explore the zero-risk trade; by definition, money invested in a zero-risk trade is not at risk. When trading stock or options, we also look at some ways to limit risk quite effectively.

What we first need to do in deciding how much money we will assign to investing or trading is to understand that we never want to put at risk anything but that portion which truly is "risk money." As an example, let us say we have $20,000. Of that $20,000, we know that we need $10,000 to pay a tuition bill in eight months and we have $5,000 earmarked for making some home improvements in six months. The remaining $5,000 is not needed for any necessity. That $5,000, then, is what I define as risk money. We could lose it all and though we certainly would not be happy about it, that loss would not put us in a position where we would be unable to pay some important bill. (I'll discuss the critically important concept of money management a bit later to show that even with $5,000 of risk money, we would not put it all at risk in a single investment or trade).

In the example, we have $5,000 of money we could risk and $15,000 we need for necessities. That doesn't mean we can only invest the $5,000; it means we could invest the whole $20,000 but put only $5,000 of the $20,000 at risk. So, as we look at this element of our business plan, we are really saying how much we have to invest and what portion of that amount we can actually put at risk.

What Are My Business Hours?

If we decided to open a retail store as our business, one of the things we would do would be to set our hours. The investing or trading business is no different in that we need to devote some time to it. One of the great things about trading is that it does not require inordinately long hours. I conduct my own trading in no more than two or three hours a day and then I am free to enjoy whatever I want. I calculate that I worked about 3,000 hours a year (60 hours a week times 50 weeks) practicing law. I now work only about 500 hours a year (2.5 hours a day times 5 days times 40 weeks). Though I work only one sixth the time I used to, the rewards have been much greater! Notice that I worked 50 weeks a year practicing law but only 40 weeks trading. That's an extra 70 full days I have free in addition to the nine and a half hours a day I no longer have to work. I have more time for family, travel, volunteering, and play than I ever had before, and I have the money to enjoy the time. At first, when I began to trade for my livelihood, I worked through a learning curve. I confess that during those days I did spend a lot more time on my trading business than I do now, but most of the additional time was devoted to study.

Though I have digressed, I believe the digression was important. The lesson, for me at least, was that I can work less, have more, and enjoy a significantly higher quality of life. The time devoted to study was definitely worth it to me.

In any event, it is very important to set your business hours. Just like any other business, those hours should be a time devoted strictly to your trading and investing. Many investors, including me, enjoy trading from home. However, while trading from home can be delightful, it can also have drawbacks. At home, the trader risks interruptions from spouse, friends, children, and neighbors. It is critical to the success of the business that you make it clear to all that the time you choose for your business hours must be devoted strictly to business. I doubt you will find many objections when you explain that this time ultimately can provide a higher quality of life for you and your family. If you cannot find uninterrupted time to conduct your business at home, find a place where you can. You might even consider renting some small office space if necessary. You are dealing with your money and with your future. You need to concentrate on your business in a quiet atmosphere—period.

Several years ago, I had a student come to me for private mentoring. As I do in those situations, I asked him whether he had a business plan, and, like most unsuccessful traders, he did not. I began taking him through the elements of a plan and tried to help him develop his own plan. When we got to setting his business hours, he had a multitude of excuses why he could not set specific hours. Interestingly, he had no other job and had decided he would be a full-time trader, yet he obstinately refused to set hours even when I let him know that, once set, he could later change them. He quit the mentoring and went back to his own devices. Last I heard, he was still an unsuccessful trader.

I relate that little episode to underscore the necessity of discipline. Good investing does require self-discipline. Anyone who is so undisciplined that they cannot even decide when they are going to devote time to their business is almost certainly doomed to fail.

Make your business hours comfortable for you and your schedule. Set them during a time when your mind will be fresh and clear, not when you are exhausted from a hard day at your other job. Realize that your business hours do not have to be daily. Your hours could be on a Saturday morning or a Sunday afternoon. The quality of the hours spent is infinitely more important than the quantity.

I have a close friend who traveled extensively and often out of the country for his job. We were discussing his investment business hours and he told me he just could not look at the markets each day, or even once a week because of his demanding schedule. I asked him whether he had a specific time once a month when he could attend to his investment business and he said that would not be a problem. Well, that is what he did until his retirement. There are many ways that orders can be placed and safety nets erected even if the investor can look at his business only once a month. That is what my friend did until he was able to retire from his job. Now, he has set different hours in keeping with his new lifestyle.

The point is simply that any investor needs to treat his investing business as just that, a business. Part time or full time is fine. Part time can be once a day, once a week, once a month, or, yes, even once a year using the appropriate strategy. When the business hours are selected, the real goal is that the time spent be quiet, uninterrupted, and with singular concentrated devotion to the business.

What Strategies Will I Employ?

Later in the book, we'll explore a number of specific strategies in detail. Each of them can be profitable, but you might pick only one or two for your trading plan. Right now, I just want to give you some general guidelines to help you select the specific strategies you include in your plan.

Three factors are worthy of consideration when deciding what strategy or strategies to employ in your investing or trading. First, the strategies you choose should be ones that you know well. While that sounds obvious, I have seen traders who have recently been exposed to a strategy that is new to them jump right on the bandwagon and start trading the strategy immediately. I would suggest that any trader paper trade a strategy for some time before using real money. Paper trading is simply keeping a careful and honest record of when you would enter a position, the debit or credit at entry (including commissions) and when you would exit the position, then recording the ultimate gain or loss. Some brokerage sites actually provide the ability to record such "virtual trades," but no matter how you do it, paper trading will help you gain an understanding of the strategy with which you are experimenting before putting real money at risk. If you find that you are losing money on your paper trades, you would not want to trade that strategy with real money until you could improve upon those results. If the strategy does well on paper, you may then consider making some small real-money trades as you become more and more comfortable. It is also important to recognize that the transition from paper trading to real-money trading can be difficult. It is easy to keep the emotions out of paper trading, but difficult to keep them at bay when risking your cash. Keep in mind that what you were doing while you were paper trading actually worked so do not change it. It is amazing how many people do well when paper trading and then change what they have been doing when they put real money at risk. Instead of deviating from what you have already proven to work, start with small trades as you gradually build confidence with your real-money trades. Once you know and fully understand a strategy, you can add it to your plan; just make sure you test it by first paper trading and then by risking only small amounts as you transition to trading the new strategy with real money.

The second factor in deciding what strategies to include in your plan is whether you actually like trading the specific strategy. Some strategies are simply more appealing than others to any individual trader. You may find, for example, that you prefer buying options over buying stock or selling stock short, or you may find just the opposite. I am talking about your personality here. If you do not enjoy trading a particular strategy, you are probably better off using something different. In trading, there are many ways to achieve success, so you might as well select a way that you enjoy.

The third factor is your risk tolerance. I have already mentioned risk and risk tolerance a number of times. Here, again, it is your personal risk tolerance that becomes a guide for the strategies you will choose. In this book, much of my emphasis is on utilizing strategies that let the investor sleep soundly at night. As far as I know, there is no perfect strategy. Each strategy involves some compromise between risk and reward. Generally, the more limited the risk, the more likely the reward will be limited as well. Conversely, when the risk is high, the theoretical reward may be higher as well.

As we go forward and discuss various strategies in depth, we'll see specifically how risk and reward interrelate. Consider, for example, the most common strategy of simply buying a stock with the hope that it will go up and can then be sold at a profit. What is the risk of the strategy of buying a stock? It is the price of the stock. For every dollar the stock drops, the shareholder loses a dollar. If the stock goes to zero, the total investment is lost. In that sense, buying a stock can be very risky. If you do not believe that can happen, think back to one-time high flyers like Enron and WorldCom. Even strong companies with deservedly solid reputations can take big tumbles. Just looking at some of the Dow 30 Industrials, we can see some of the risks inherent in simply buying a stock.

In May 2001, for example, an investor could have purchased Alcoa, Inc. (AA) at $45 a share and seen it lose more that half of its value by the latter part of 2002. In fact, even as late as the last quarter of 2006, AA remained well below the May 2001 high. I do not mean to pick on Alcoa. It is a fine company, but we must realize that just because a company is strong or well known does not mean it is a good stock to buy. AT&T (T) sold for as high as $58 at the end of November 2000, but plummeted to around $20 by September 2002. As of this writing it has not approached the high in 2000. The behemoth General Electric (GE) hit over $59 in September 2000, and after a big dip only got back to the mid-$30s six years later. The point is that even the biggest and best companies' stock can have significant risk when the strategy is simply to buy the stock with the hope it will go up and the investor can later sell at a profit.

The other side of the strategy of buying stock and later selling is that the potential gain is theoretically unlimited. For every dollar the stock moves up, the investor gains a dollar a share (on paper at least). The gain is realized when the stock is ultimately sold. Here, again, there are many examples of tremendous upward movements in stock. NVIDIA Corporation (NVDA), on a split-adjusted basis, went from $4 in September 2002 to over $30 four years later. Akamai Technologies (AKAM) traded at $0.60 in October 2002 and was trading at more than $50 a share four years later. Many examples of similar great bullish moves exist.

Every investor needs to be aware of the risk of the strategies he or she employs. There is nothing wrong with a high-risk/high-reward strategy if the trader knows that is what a particular strategy encompasses. However, a low-risk/high-reward strategy might make that same trader much more comfortable. You might prefer a zero-risk/moderate-reward strategy. Whatever the case, choose the strategies best suited to your personal risk tolerance.

I would like to offer one last thought on strategies in general. Do not feel that you have to use a lot of different strategies. It is much better to know one well than many only partially. If you have a strategy for an upward-moving market, a flat market, and a downward-moving market, what else do you need? Is there any other direction a market can go? Actually, you do not even need as many as three strategies to make a lot of money. If you know one strategy well and know when to use it, you should do very well.

When Will I Make My Trading Decisions?

Remember the era of the day trader? During the latter part of the 1990s the markets were soaring, and Fed Chairman Alan Greenspan warned of "irrational exuberance." Traders went to brokerage houses every day and entered and exited positions during the day. The rule often was that all trades had to be closed by market close. Some traders were enormously margined. In other words, they were borrowing heavily from the broker to enter extremely highly leveraged trades. As the markets rocketed upward, many made fortunes. Euphoria ruled. Then, the markets turned and losses began. For many, the euphoria was replaced by anxiety; losses mounted and anxiety turned to abject fear. Noses were pressed closer and closer to the computer screens and many lost everything.

Is that the way you would like to trade? One of the greatest enemies to successful trading is emotion. If we own a stock that is rising and it has a down day, many of us will sell because we are afraid it will continue down. Fear makes the decision. We may fail to see that the stock is still in a strong uptrend and that the little drop was on slight volume. Fear takes us out, and the next day we watch as the stock resumes its upward march. We have cut our profits. Or we may get into a stock that we "feel" is going to go up. Instead, it immediately turns down. We decide we will hold because we just became a buy-and-hold investor. The stock drops $5 and we say to ourselves: "If it just gets back to where I bought it, I'll sell." It drops some more and we say: "It's coming back. If it just goes back up to the $5 loss, I'll sell it."

What is happening? Our emotion has taken control of the investment decisions. We are now letting our losses run. We are afraid of losing, but greed stops us from taking the loss and moving on. We just want to get some of it back. It is even worse when we are looking at a computer screen and watching the real time ticks up and down. Notice what we are doing. We are cutting our profits and letting our losses run. Why? We do exactly the opposite of what we should be doing because we are reacting emotionally and in the heat of battle.

My suggestion is that you decide to make your trading decisions when the battle is not engaged. Make the decisions, for example, when the market is closed. Choose a time when you can evaluate what you are doing rationally. Look at the company, look at the chart, and decide whether it is a position that you would want to enter and then decide the price at which you would be willing to enter. If you are buying, decide the maximum price at which you will purchase. Decide precisely what will trigger your purchase (perhaps a new high or a bounce up off a moving average, etc.). At the same time, decide exactly what price will trigger your exit if the stock moves against you. Decide how you will move your exit up as the stock moves up.

After you have made all those decisions, you have nothing left to do but put them into effect when the triggers are hit. All—I repeat, *all*—of your decisions will have been made before you ever enter the position. The decisions will not have been made under the excitement of a moving market, and they will not have been driven by emotion.

The simple act of making trading decisions at a time when you can contemplate what you are doing rationally will help you discipline your trading. A disciplined trader is much more likely to be a winner than one who trades in response to the emotions generated by a moving market. Make the time you will make decisions part of your trading plan and then stick to the plan.

What Is the Maximum Number of Trades to Have in Place at One Time?

Once again, this is a question that only you will be able to answer. If you are new to trading, the number should probably be low. It can be very easy to lose track if you have a high number of trades open at one time. Even advanced traders may have a very limited number of trades in place at one time. I once had a student who left her employment and became a successful trader. She held only a single position at a time.

My best suggestion is to err on the side of having too few rather than too many trades working at one time. The number of open trades will be influenced by the strategy or strategies you are using. Though we have not yet looked at specific strategies, it should be fairly obvious that some strategies will require more babysitting than others. The zero-risk trade, for example, does not need to be watched constantly, while a credit spread may need closer observation and even adjustment. The key is to be comfortable with the number of open positions you have at any one time. Some of us may have no trouble managing 10 positions, while others may find that four or five are too taxing.

Money management, too, plays a significant role in the number of outstanding trades. I never want to risk more on any one trade or in the total of my overall positions than my money management plan permits.

How Will I Make My Trading Decisions?

So far, we have discussed the who (you), what (selecting strategies), when, and where, of your trading plan. Now we need to address the "how" and "why" to complete the general guidelines for your plan. The "why" is pretty easy, at least superficially. We trade to make money. While that reason may be overly simplistic, it should suffice for now as we turn to the important decisions of how you plan to trade.

When I talk about how to trade, I mean how you go about your decision making before you enter a trade and how you decide where and under what specific circumstances you will exit the trade. In a sense, I am putting the cart before the horse because I have not yet detailed the strategies and tactics that can be used to reduce risk in trading, but I want to be sure you include a section in your trading plan that does set out how you are going to go about actually trading. The new trader may want to skip this section for now and return to it after I have explained the specific strategies designed to reduce or remove risk later in the book. In any event, the nuts and bolts of "how" I do it will be coming later.

There are two distinct types of pure traders: *fundamental traders* and *technical traders*. Fundamental traders try to gather all the facts about a company. They want to know as much as possible about what it does, its capitalization, debt, revenue, earnings, growth, price-to-earnings ratio, return on assets, return on equity, percentage of shares held by insiders, percentage of shares held by institutions, net income, free cash flow, and so on. The fundamental investor may also want to know as much as possible about the management team and what analysts' recommendations may be regarding the company. Having gathered as much of that information as possible, the fundamental trader decides whether to buy the stock.

I see at least three problems with the purely fundamental approach: (1) it is extremely difficult to gather and analyze all the information; (2) it fails to address the question of when to buy the stock; and (3) the fundamental approach often is unable to react quickly enough to changes in the fundamentals themselves. None of those criticisms is to say that the pure fundamental approach cannot be successful. All we need to do is look at the astonishing results achieved by Warren Buffett to see the pinnacle to which a pure fundamental investor can rise. At the same time, however, fundamentals can change in the blink of an eye. A competitor may announce a new product that makes our company's product obsolete (do you still use a typewriter or carbon paper or a record player?). The CFO may be caught with his hand in the cookie jar, or the CEO might be arrested. Any of those scenarios would certainly change the fundamentals of a company.

Pure technical traders, conversely, are completely unconcerned with the fundamentals of a company. They place their trades based on chart formations using price, volume, and, perhaps some other indicators to make their decisions. Though some critics argue that technicians are only expecting history to repeat itself, technical analysis is more than that. It is true that certain chart formations tend to provide a clue to future stock price movement. Double bottoms often foretell a movement back up, just as double tops, for example, may be accurate in predicting a downturn. No formation, however, is infallible. The real value that I see in technical trading is that it provides the trader with an artificial device through which to discipline trading. The value of such a device is that it removes the emotion from entries and, even more importantly, exits. Technical analysis can indeed provide information about the "when" of entry and exit that fundamental analysis does not.

I am closer to being a technical trader than I am to being a fundamental trader. At times, my trades have been completely technical. I have entered based solely upon some indication on a chart without any regard to fundamentals. I confess that I have entered positions without even knowing the whole name of the company and having no idea what it does. I have made a fair amount of money on pure technical trades. The beauty of technical trading, in my mind, is that you always have a disciplined entry and a disciplined exit. You can make a decision where to enter based, for example, on a moving average line. Suppose a stock moves up from below the 50-day moving average and breaks above that average, as we can see in Figure 3.1. We could enter a bullish position. Our exit would be a violation of that same 50-day moving average. As long as the stock is moving up, the line formed by the moving average would be moving up as well. If the stock stays above the moving average, we know that it is continuing in the direction we want it to go. If the price falls below the moving average, the stock is no longer in the same uptrend, so we can exit. The danger of emotion has been removed.

In the example in Figure 3.1, the stock price broke above the 50-day moving average in October 2005, at which point we could have entered. It stayed above that same 50-day moving average until April 2006, at which time we would have a signal to exit. The entry price would have been in the area of $30, and the exit around $50. Thus, we would have enjoyed a gain of about $20 a share and would have simply followed a disciplined exit, that is, a break of the same moving average line we had chosen for our entry

I should note that this book is not intended to be a course on technical analysis. There is a plethora of material on the subject, and the serious investor should take the time to learn the basics at least. I will, however, rely on some charts as we go forward to demonstrate some of the principles I consider to be important in making entry and exit decisions.

One of the major purposes of this book is to illustrate methods of trading that reduce risk. When I seek reduced-risk trades in buying a stock, I tend to combine some fundamental analysis with a technical entry and exit. If I am bullish (which I would be buying a stock), I do look at the company. I am particularly interested in seeing that it has good earnings in recent time and as compared to the same period(s) in the past. I also want to be sure there is some institutional ownership, but not so much that it is overpowering. I like to see at least 5 percent but no more than about 60 percent institutional ownership. I prefer a company that does not have a great deal of debt, particularly when compared to other companies in the same industry.

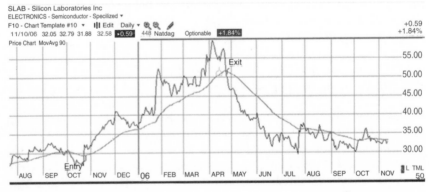

FIGURE 3.1 Entry and Exit with Moving Average. (Telechart 2005® chart courtesy of Worden Brothers, Inc.)

Once I have satisfied myself that the company is reasonably strong, I then search for a good technical entry, meaning one where I have an exit that is close to my initial entry and one that is clearly defined by some technical line. If I find that kind of entry, I am willing to buy the stock. My exit is predefined. It may be based on a movement down that violates the same technical line I chose to signal my entry (as in Figure 3.1). In most circumstances, the worst that will happen is that I can get out with a relatively small loss. At the same time, it can keep me in a position that is moving in my desired direction until the stock reverses. The method helps cut my losses and lets my profits run.

In order to make these decisions, I need some fundamental information on the stock. Usually, that fundamental information can be found on your brokerage web site or through your broker. In order to make the entry and exit decisions, you will need some knowledge of technical analysis and a charting service.

Once those tools are available to you, you will be able to construct the "how" part of your plan. Now you can decide what chart or charts to use in your decision-making process. Perhaps you will want to look at the market every day. If that is the case, you may decide to make your final decisions regarding entries and exits based on a daily chart. However, if your plan is to have business hours only once a week, you may not want to make decisions based on a daily chart, but might, instead, choose a weekly chart to find entries and exits. Dr. Alexander Elder, in his excellent book, *Come into My Trading Room* (John Wiley & Sons, 2002), for example, reviews his "Triple Screen Method," which utilizes different time frames and indicators in reaching a decision. Later on, I'll show you some of the methods I use to choose my own entries.

Hopefully, as you continue to gain understanding, you will develop your own method. Most importantly, you need to plan how you are going to go about making your trading decisions before you actually make the decisions. You want to have a process to follow that takes you to the ultimate action of buying or selling.

How Will I Enter and How Will I Exit?

One of the most serious issues traders consider is when to get into and out of positions. Too often, these decisions are based purely on emotion. Your plan should include your method for entry and exit so that the trade will be conducted in a disciplined fashion. Your goal is to enter the trade at a point where your likelihood of success is great and any loss you may have to take will be limited and within the parameters of the risk you decided to take before you entered the position.

I am a great believer in making all decisions before ever entering a trade. If you have every decision made before entry, you will not be influenced by the minute-to-minute, hour-to-hour, or day-to-day price fluctuations of the stock. All you will have to do is implement the decisions you made in the first place. Earlier, I referred to Figure 3.1 as an example of using a moving average as both entry and exit criteria. In that case, before ever making the trade, a hypothetical trader would have made it part of his plan that he would enter when a stock broke above the 50-day moving average and he would exit when it broke below the 50-day moving average. Simple, isn't it? All our trader had to do was wait until the stock went above the 50-day moving average and then buy the stock. When would he get out?

The hypothetical plan said to get out when the stock went below the 50-day moving average. In the example, our trader would have suffered only a small loss (unless the stock gapped down) had the price turned down shortly after entry. However, the price moved up. Can you see the temptation of selling as soon as the stock moved up $5 or $10? Waiting until the predetermined exit (a break below the 50-day moving average) was hit enabled profits to run and would have resulted in a much greater gain than emotions may have tempted the trader to take.

Please understand that I am not advocating any specific entry/exit method. I only want you to see how helpful having such a method can be. Can the moving average work? Yes, it can if a stock trends. If the stock moves back and forth in a fairly tight range, the result can be a whipsaw in and out of the position until the stock's direction is ultimately determined. Whipsaws can chew up some commissions, even though commissions are so reduced over what they were in the not-so-distant past.

There are many other examples of ways to enter and exit positions. I'll show a couple shortly. What I believe is most important, however, is that the entry is really determined by where you set your *initial* exit. When I refer to the initial exit, I mean the exit you are going to use if the stock turns against you shortly after entry. Yes, I think that initial exit is what determines entry. Exit is determined by risk tolerance, and no matter who you may be, you want to keep risk minimized. The entry, therefore, should be relatively close to your *initial* exit and certainly no farther away than your predetermined risk. In other words, do not enter a position where your initial exit is too far away. If you are wrong on the direction, you do not want to suffer an uncomfortably large loss. Your initial exit, if you were wrong on direction, needs to be close to your entry. Your initial exit also needs to be clear. As I said before, the clarity comes from a technical approach. It can be the violation of a moving average, a violation of a trend line, a change in an indicator, or a signal from something like a Japanese candlestick chart formation.

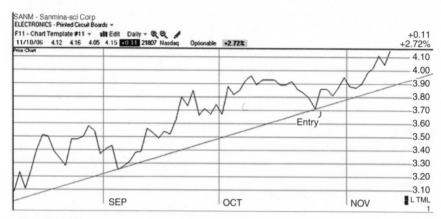

FIGURE 3.2 Trend Entry. (Telechart 2005® chart courtesy of Worden Brothers, Inc.)

Figures 3.2 through 3.4 illustrate some ways to set entries based on nearby exits.

In Figure 3.2, we can see that the stock was trending up and bounced up off the uptrend in the latter part of October. That bounce provided a potential entry point using the trend line as both an entry and exit. The entry would have been in the area of $3.80. Had the stock turned down

FIGURE 3.3 Entry and Exit Using MACD Crossover. (Telechart 2005® chart courtesy of Worden Brothers, Inc.)

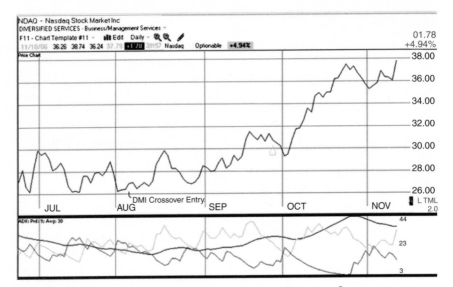

FIGURE 3.4 DMI Crossover Entry and Exit. (Telechart 2005® chart courtesy of Worden Brothers, Inc.)

shortly after entry and broken through the line, the trader using the line as an *initial* exit would probably have sold the position around $3.70 for a small loss. As it turned out, the trader would still be in the position as the stock continued to climb. Only when the line was finally broken would the trader exit.

Once the trade became profitable, the trader could move stop loss orders up behind the move or even draw a steeper trend line connecting the low point near entry to the low in mid-November and thereby protect additional profit. In any case, the trader would be making those decisions at a time of calm, rather than during the emotionally charged times when the market is moving.

Another possibility for determining entries and exits used by some traders is an indicator crossover. Moving average convergence divergence (MACD), stochastics, and the Directional Movement Index (DMI) are some examples of indicators used by some traders to enter and exit positions. Of course, there is no reason that indicators such as these cannot be used in conjunction with chart formations such as those discussed earlier. For example a positive MACD crossover as a stock comes off a double (or multiple) bottom may give added reason to enter a bullish position and a negative MACD crossover at a double (or multiple) top could provide reason to exit a position. Figure 3.3 shows an example of an entry and an exit suggested by the crossover of the MACD histogram in the lower window of the chart. Here, the entry was suggested around $38 and the exit just short of $42.

Figure 3.4 shows an entry based on a DMI crossover. As can be seen in the lower window and ignoring the relatively smooth line, when the more uneven (faster) line crosses above the somewhat smoother (slower) line, there was an entry. In September, the faster line crossed briefly below the slower and then moved back above it. Strict adherence to the plan would have resulted in an exit and then reentry a day or so later. That action would have resulted in a little whipsaw, but would have been of little consequence in this example.

These illustrations are just that—illustrations. They are designed to show a few ways a trader could decide upon entries and exits. The key is that you choose a plan for entry and exit for each trade and that the decision regarding a close, clear initial exit be made before the trade is entered. Incorporating those decisions into your own plan will definitely help you reduce the worry factor in any trade.

What Indicators Will I Use?

In the preceding sections, I mentioned MACD, stochastics, and DMI. They are each individual indicators. In general, MACD and DMI are helpful in confirming that a trend is in place. Stochastics, however, may be more helpful as a momentum indicator, helping to determine overbought and oversold levels. There are innumerable indicators, and more are being devised each year. None is perfect. Each is derived mathematically and cannot completely account for emotion, which is a significant element in market movement.

In my estimation, the most important information is still price and volume. Indicators can be helpful in confirming what we see in the price and volume movements and can suggest direction or reversals of direction. I would suggest that you select a small number of indicators that you like and limit your use of indicators to those few. Attempting to use a vast array of indicators simultaneously can be confusing and counterproductive. Remember, they are only aids in the decision-making process.

Another useful device is Japanese candlestick charting. I have found that knowledge of the candlesticks has improved my trading significantly. You may want to study this charting method and consider incorporating it in your own trading plan. I have concluded that certain candlestick formations, particularly in areas of support and resistance, are extremely valuable in predicting reversals. Steve Nison's *Japanese Candlestick Charting* (Prentice Hall, 1991) and *The Candlestick Course* (John Wiley & Sons, 2003) are excellent introductions to this powerful trading tool.

What Types of Orders Will I Use?

When buying to enter a position, I suggest you always use a limit order as distinguished from a market order. A limit order specifies that you will pay up to a specified amount. You may get it for less, but you will not pay more than the limit you set. A limit order is distinguished from a market order in that a market order means you will pay whatever the market is asking at the time your order hits the floor. Unless you specify otherwise, orders are market orders.

The following story, whether fable or not, illustrates the danger of buying on market orders: Several years ago, there was a news story that a cure for a particular type of cancer had been discovered by a publicly traded company. A lady heard the news and called her broker and placed an order to buy 1,000 shares of the stock that had been trading for about $25 a share. Since she did not place a limit order, her order went to the floor as a market order. Obviously, the news of a cancer cure generated a great deal of interest in the company and the stock quickly became the subject of many buy orders. The price skyrocketed. By the time the lady's order was filled, the stock price was around $88 a share. She was filled around that amount, though she thought she was buying it for about $25. Unfortunately, the news story was incorrect. Someone had misinterpreted information that the company had announced weeks earlier. In fact, there was no cure for cancer yet found. The stock tumbled even below the $25 to around $23. The effect on the lady was that she thought she was buying 1,000 shares of stock for $25 ($25,000). She actually bought the stock at $88 ($88,000) because she had placed a market order, and then had to sell at $23 ($23,000). The result of placing a market order instead of a limit order was a $65,000 loss in one day! The moral of the story is clear: Use limit orders when buying.

As I hope I have emphasized sufficiently, exits are absolutely critical. You do not have a complete result until you are out of the trade. We have already discussed exit strategy, but now we must consider how we will actually implement that strategy. My observations lead me to conclude that many investors have a great deal of difficulty closing a trade. Fear or greed takes over and they either fail to cut losses or they cut profits prematurely. Many a trader has said to himself something like: "I'll get out if my stock drops 2 percent (or 3 percent or $1 or some specific amount) from my entry price." The stock then drops that amount and they stay in, arguing that "it will come back." Nothing gives me the shivers more than the phrase: "It will come back." Sure, it may come back, but if you established an exit, use it. Now, at least, the loss is cut. If it does come back, there is nothing to prevent you from taking another position in the same stock.

Hopefully, your plan already contains an exit strategy that is in place before you ever enter a trade. Now the issue is how to implement that strategy. I have heard many traders say that they will close the trade when the stock drops below their predetermined exit only to hang on with the "it will come back" philosophy. If you find you cannot be faithful to your exit, set a stop loss order. If you own a stock, a stop loss order is an order to your broker that tells the broker to sell the stock in the event the price hits a certain level. Stop loss orders are usually placed so that they are good until canceled. (Check with your individual brokerage because "good 'til canceled" may mean 30 days or 60 days to them.)

Say you own XYZ stock at $45 and you decided before you entered that you would exit if the stock went below $44. You could place a sell stop at $44 good until canceled. That would mean your position would automatically be sold if the stock hit $44 or below. Does that mean you would get $44 no matter what? No, it means that once your stock price hit $44, a market order to sell your stock would be immediately placed. If the stock is trading around $44, that is probably what you would get. But suppose the stock closed at $48 the night before and before market open the company announced some horrendous news. The next morning the stock opens at $40. In that case, your stop would have been hit because the stock was below $44, but it would be sold at the market. Is that a bad thing? Probably not. You want to be out of the position since the likelihood is that it will fall even farther. The stop loss has helped you cut your losses.

A stop loss order is also a good idea if you cannot be watching the market. If the stock turns against you, you will automatically be taken out. Suppose you are on a cruise and are unable to follow the market every day. With a stop loss in place, you can be confident that your position will be closed if something untoward occurs even though you are completely unaware of what is happening to the stock. In a sense, you have put the stock on autopilot. Some brokerage firms even permit a trailing stop loss. A trailing stop loss can be set as a percentage or a dollar amount. As the stock goes higher, the trailing stop automatically moves up and is recalculated on each higher tick. As an aside, I like trailing stops, but usually place them only when the position has already become profitable. I should note that there is no charge to change a stop loss order. In fact, in my own trading, I often move up my stop loss orders in an effort to capture more and more profit as the stock moves my way.

Like anything else, stop loss orders have a downside as well as benefits. One downside is that stops may be visible to the floor. It has happened that a stock will drop, hitting a price that triggers a number of stops, and then turn back up. That scenario can be very frustrating, and some traders do not want to place stops for that reason. An alternative is to set alerts with your broker or charting service. When a specific price you set is hit, you will get an alert on your screen, by e-mail, or through a cell phone. You then can take a look and see if the market is turning back up. The problem remains that even if they receive an alert, many traders will not act. Of course, if you are on the cruise, the alert may be of little value in any event.

In formulating your plan, I suggest that you include a provision that you buy on limit orders only. In implementing exits, you have several choices. I suggest you choose the method that will assure that you will actually act when your predetermined exit is reached.

What Are Your Specific Trading Expectancies?

Your trading business plan should include your expectancies. What return do you expect? Make this element reasonable and one against which you can measure your actual performance. If you have paper traded strategies before using actual money, you should have a basis upon which to rely in setting reasonable expectations. Understand that some trades will not meet expectations and others will exceed them. Return to this section of your plan at reasonable intervals and see how you are doing.

YOUR PLAN IS ALWAYS A WORK IN PROGRESS

Your investing plan should be a living document, not something carved forever in granite. Think of the plan as something written in disappearing ink to be revised and rewritten as you change. One day, for example, you may find that trading has brought you more wealth than you imagined. You may decide to go from part-time to full-time trading as I did. As you gain knowledge and experience, you may prefer newly tested strategies over ones you used in the past.

As we grow older, our risk tolerance often changes. If you are young, you may choose riskier strategies looking for greater returns. As you add years, lower-risk or no-risk strategies may have greater appeal. At some stage you may be zealously accumulating capital, while at a different stage you may be more in agreement with Will Rogers, who once said: "I am more interested in the return of my capital than I am in the return on my capital."

MONEY MANAGEMENT

Few things are more important to the success of an investor or trader than good money management. An acquaintance of mine studied trading a bit and began trading real money. He was very successful at first. In fact, he called almost daily to tell me how well he was doing and how much he was making. Then, one day, the calls stopped. After a few days, I called him to find out how he was doing. "Not very well," he reported, "I lost almost all my trading money." I asked what happened and he told me he had successfully traded a position in a particular stock option several times. Each trade made more than the previous one. He enjoyed five successful trades in a row on that one stock. On the sixth trade he invested all his capital. In effect, he "bet it all on black." You can probably guess what happened. The stock, which had been behaving in a very bullish fashion, gapped down several dollars at the open one day and his option position became essentially worthless. He was out of the game forever.

The stock and options markets seem to have an uncanny way of humbling us. Just about the time we think we have it figured out, Murphy's Law takes effect. The trade we thought was so wonderful turns on us and shows us we do not control the markets. Knowing that, how can we avoid the fate of my acquaintance? If we are to be successful, we must stay in the game, and the only way to stay in the game is to manage our money carefully.

Money management is undoubtedly one of the most important factors in successful investing. A number of writers and successful traders have shared their thoughts on money management. Among them, Dr. Alexander Elder in *Come into My Trading Room* sets out his 2 percent and 6 percent rules. In *How to Make Money in Stocks* (3rd edition, McGraw-Hill, 2003), William J. O'Neil speaks about cutting a loss when a stock is 7 or 8 percent below the price you paid. Though each successful trader may have a variation on his or her specific money management plan, one dare not miss the point that each does have a money management plan. Without such a plan, the investor's chance of success is very significantly reduced.

In my classes, I teach the necessity of money management; the necessity of keeping in the game. What I tell my students is that they should consider risking either roughly equal dollar amounts or a set percentage (perhaps 3 to 5 percent). I believe that risking a set percentage is far preferable, but those with limited risk money might find it very difficult to trade equal percentages since they simply would not have enough cash. Someone new to trading, for example, might have only $1,000 to trade. Three percent of that $1,000 would be only $30, and it is almost impossible to find a $30 trade including commissions. For an investor with such limited funds, the choices become either (1) wait until you have more money to risk, or (2) trade equal dollar amounts. The person with a $1,000 bankroll may consider making $200 trades, which could be accomplished with some option positions. Naturally, the preferred course would be to paper trade until more risk money is accumulated and then trade where relatively small equal percentages are risked.

My personal rule of thumb (where I enter trades with risk) is to invest roughly 3 percent of my account in each trade. As the value of the account fluctuates, so, too, does the size of my trade. As you recall from my earlier discussion, I also limit the number of trades I have in place at any one time so that I can keep track of what is going on in each position. I am never fully invested and try to keep about 30 percent of my account in zero-risk or nearly zero-risk trades. I also usually keep anywhere from 15 to 25 percent in cash in the event I come upon some opportunity or in the event I need cash in some emergency. Using those figures and a hypothetical account of $500,000, the result would be about $125,000 in cash, $150,000 in zero-risk (or nearly so) trades, and about $15,000 devoted to each risk trade.

Under those circumstances, the investor could have up to 15 active trades. In fact, though I often have as many as 15 active trades, I believe that is more than the average part-time trader should try to follow at one time. When I write about $15,000 devoted to each risk trade, I do not mean to suggest that the whole $15,000 is likely to be at real risk. As I noted in the section on orders, stop loss orders would likely be placed that would result in exiting the position well in advance of almost any devastating loss.

The bottom line is to adopt a money management strategy that will keep you in the game. Check out the approaches suggested by people like William O'Neil and Dr. Elder. See if my own method is something that appeals to you, but unless you are a pure gambler (and this book is not meant for the gambler), do not bet it all on one play. While it is certainly possible to make a lot of money on a gamble, it is much more likely that you can increase your wealth steadily using sound principles of money management. The gambler, like my acquaintance, may ultimately lose it all. The investor who employs money management principles will lose on some trades but, overall, has a much greater chance of success.

CONTINUE YOUR INVESTING EDUCATION

It has always astonished me that in the United States there is such a great emphasis on making money, yet almost no class or school teaches us how to make money. Schools teach us how to get jobs and how to perform those jobs with the underlying premise that by gaining employment and doing a job we will make money. To a limited extent, and a limited extent only, that is true. Almost no job, though, leads to wealth. A job may lead to some financial comfort and at least to some perceived security, but it rarely leads to financial independence. If we are to gain financial independence and wealth, we need to learn how to make money. One of the ways to do that is to learn how to be a successful investor.

Investing skills can be learned and can be improved. Since sound investing and trading skills can provide us with additional income, a better quality of life, a more secure retirement, and the ability to do what we want when we want, as well as increase our wealth, it seems to me that it is worth the effort to learn as much as we can about them.

Exactly what should we be doing? I think it is important to learn some basic strategies thoroughly and then to learn new strategies. There are many resources for us to increase our knowledge. Books, seminars, DVDs, CDs, brokerage web sites, and organizations like the various exchanges and the Options Industry Council all offer opportunities for us to advance our abilities. Time spent honing and increasing our trading and investment skills can yield rewards far beyond the effort. Appendix E includes a list of resources that have been helpful to me. Quite simply, trading has changed my life. Even after trading and investing successfully for many years, I always include some study time each week.

As we gain knowledge, we not only learn basic strategies and improve our methods, but we can also learn adjustments to trades that enable us to sweeten some of those that have gone sour. If you enjoy trading and see the extraordinary changes possible in your life, I urge you to continue your education.

Now, as my classes insist—on to the good stuff.

CHAPTER 4

How Put Options Can Protect Your Money, and Also Make You Money

Puts are a type of option that can be used in several very important ways. This chapter will cover both the protective put and directional puts. The protective put is a form of "insurance policy" for stocks you may own. Directional puts may be purchased to make money when there is a downward move in a stock, sector, or market, or they may be sold to generate income when the stock, sector, or market is rising. Before getting into the meat of these strategies, it is important to understand some of the terminology.

DEFINING THE KEY TERMS

In order to proceed, we need to explore options a little bit. Options are contracts that give the buyer certain rights and place certain obligations upon the seller. When we enter an option contract, we almost never know with whom we have contracted. We do not need to be concerned with who is on the other side of the option contract since the contract is guaranteed by the Option Clearing Corporation. All we need to know is that if we are the buyer of an option, we have certain rights. If we are the seller of an option, we have undertaken certain obligations. We do not have to worry about the enforcement of our rights since they are guaranteed by an independent organization. Table 4.1 identifies the rights and obligations of buyers and sellers of calls and puts.

TABLE 4.1 Option Trader Rights and Obligations

Action	Rights	Obligations
Buying calls	Right to buy stock at the strike price anytime before expiration	
Selling calls		Must sell stock at strike price before expiration if assigned (called) before options expire
Buying puts	The right to force someone to buy stock at the strike price before expiration	
Selling puts		Must buy stock at the strike price if assigned (put) before expiration

Generally, an option contract controls 100 shares of stock. Occasionally, an option contract controls a different number than 100 shares. Such a situation might arise, for example, when a stock has split 3:2. For that reason, you should always check before buying or selling an option contract to make certain that you know how many shares actually will be controlled by the contract.

An option is defined by four separate criteria: (1) the identity of the underlying stock; (2) the strike price; (3) the expiration date; (4) whether the option is a put or call. Many, though not all, stocks have options. The stocks that do have options are generally those that trade more heavily. Naturally, the trader should always check to see whether the stock he is trading does have options.

Strike Price

The strike price (sometimes called striking price) is the price at which the option can be exercised. For stocks priced below $30 or $35, the strike prices are generally $2.50 apart. For example, there may be strikes available at $2.50, $5, $7.50, etc. Stocks that trade above $35 in price generally have strikes that are $5 apart such as $25, $30, $35, etc. Higher-priced stocks usually have their strikes $10 apart. Those guidelines are not set in stone, so you will always want to check the option chain to see what strikes are available for the stock and options that interest you.

I should also note that some stocks such as the Nasdaq 100 Index tracking stock (QQQQ) and the Diamonds (DIA) have strikes that are only $1 apart. I'll have a great deal to say about exchange-traded funds (ETFs) like QQQQ and DIA later.

In-, At-, or Out-of-the-Money   Strike prices are often referred to as *at-the-money*, *in-the-money*, and *out-of-the-money*. Often, these terms are confusing to traders, especially those who are unfamiliar with options. If a stock is trading at $50, both the $50 call and the $50 put are at-the-money. The at-the-money option is the strike nearest the price at which the stock is currently trading.

An option is considered to be in-the-money if it has intrinsic value. Intrinsic value is the built-in value or the part of the strike price of the option that is in-the-money. Probably the easiest way to see that is to look at a call option. Assume a stock is trading at $52 a share and we own the $50 call option. Since ownership of the call option gives us the right, but not the obligation, to buy the stock at any time up to expiration for $50 and the stock is already at $52, our call option would be $2 in-the-money. In other words, we could exercise our $50 call, buy the stock for $50, and immediately sell the stock on the open market for $52. Thus, it would have $2 built-in or intrinsic value.

A put option provides the buyer with the right, but not the obligation, to force someone else to buy the stock at the strike price. If we owned a put option at a strike price of $50, we could force someone to buy our stock at $50 a share even if it were selling for less on the open market. If we owned a put option with a $50 strike price and the stock were trading for only $48 a share, our put option would be $2 in-the-money; in other words, it would have $2 of built-in or intrinsic value.

Out-of-the-money options have no intrinsic value. Going back to the example of a call, suppose we own the $50 call option and the stock is selling on the open market for only $46 a share. We would have no reason to exercise our call option and buy the stock for $50 a share when we could buy it for $46 a share on the market. In that case, our $50 call would have no built-in or intrinsic value; it would only have time value. The same would be true if we owned a $50 put and the stock were trading at $51. We could sell our stock for $51 on the market in that instance, so we would have no reason to "put" it (assign it) to someone for only $50. It would have no intrinsic value.

The following is a summary of at-, in-, and out-of-the-money **calls**:

At-the-money = strike price closest to the current stock price.

In-the-money = strike price of the call is lower than the current stock price (e.g., a $45 call when the stock is trading at $48).

Out-of-the-money = strike price of the call is higher than the current stock price (e.g., a $50 call when the current stock price is $53).

The following summarizes at-, in-, and out-of-the-money **puts**:

At-the-money = strike price closest to the current stock price.

In-the-money = strike price of the put is higher than the current stock price (e.g., a $50 put when the stock is trading at $47).

Out-of-the-money = strike price of the put is lower than the current stock price (e.g., a $50 put when the stock is trading at $52).

Intrinsic and Time Value

Option prices consist of two elements: intrinsic value and time value. Since the buyer is buying a right that will exist until expiration (unless he sells it first), he is in a position of control for that period of time and that right to control, over time, has value in and of itself. That portion of the option price is known as the time value. Suppose we bought a $50 call option for $2.50 with expiration three months away and suppose the stock was trading at exactly $50 when we bought the option. Would there be any intrinsic value at the time of the purchase? No, there would not be any intrinsic value since we could buy the same stock on the open market for $50 or we could exercise our call option and buy the stock for $50. Under that circumstance, the $2.50 premium we paid would all be time value.

Now, let us assume that the stock rose in price over the next week or so to $54 a share and we still own the $50 call. Can you see that our call option now would have $4 in intrinsic value plus time value? It would have gone from an at-the-money option to an in-the-money option. Now our option might be worth, say, $6 ($4 intrinsic plus $2 time). Of course, as time passes, the time value of an option usually diminishes. Since there is less time left until expiration, the time portion of the option price would have less value.

Finally, consider a strike price that is out-of-the-money. Going back to the same example, we bought a $50 call option at-the-money when the stock was trading at $50. Some time passes and the price of the stock drops to $47.60. There would no longer be any intrinsic value. The premium for the option would drop since some time has passed and it has gained no intrinsic value. If we held on, the premium would eventually drop to zero as the option neared expiration. If we did not sell our option some time before expiration and it gained no intrinsic value, it would expire worthless.

Tables 4.2 and 4.3 give examples of the relationship between time value and intrinsic value.

If the preceding material is new to you, it may seem complex. If you get confused as you continue through the book, go back to these tables for a quick refresher. Remember, this is a new language for you, and you might

TABLE 4.2 Calls with Stock Price at $25

In-, At-, or Out-of-the-Money	Strike Price of Call	Total Premium	Intrinsic Portion	Time Value Portion
At-the-money	$25	$1.25	0	$1.25
In-the-money	$20	$5.75	$5	$0.75
Out-of-the money	$30	$0.50	0	$0.50

need a little repetition for it to sink in completely. Believe me, the study you are performing now will definitely be worth it very soon. Right now, just remember that the premium you pay for an at-the-money or an out-of-the-money option is for time value only. The premium for an in-the-money option consists of both intrinsic value and time value. Also remember that you pay the highest premium for the time value portion of an option when you buy at-the-money options.

Expiration

For all intents and purposes, the expiration of American-style options occurs at the *close* of market on the third Friday of the month. Technically, expiration actually occurs at noon on the Saturday following the third Friday of the month. However, for the retail trader, the close of business on the third Friday is the effective expiration. Most equity (stock) options have American-style expirations and can be exercised *at any time* before expiration. European-style options cannot be exercised until expiration. While most stocks have American-style expirations, many indexes have European-style expirations. In some cases an index option may be settled on a cash basis calculated upon the *opening* price on the third Friday of the month. While these European-style options may not be exercised until expiration, they may be traded up until expiration.

TABLE 4.3 Puts with Stock Price at $25

In-, At-, or Out-of-the-Money	Strike Price of Put	Total Premium	Intrinsic Portion	Time Value Portion
At-the-money	$25	$1.00	0	$1.00
In-the-money	$30	$5.40	$5	$0.40
Out-of-the-money	$20	$0.25	0	$0.25

HOW PUTS ARE USED

The buyer of an option must pay the seller a premium. For paying that premium, the buyer obtains the rights we will begin to discuss shortly. The seller receives the premium and, as a consequence of obtaining that payment, undertakes the obligation.

Earlier, I began a discussion of the elements comprising the price of a premium of the two types of options: puts and calls. In this chapter, I'll be emphasizing the put and ways the put can be used to reduce risk as well as to make money. To reiterate, a put is a type of option wherein the buyer obtains the right, but does not have the obligation, to assign (sell) his stock to a seller of the put at the strike price anytime before expiration, and pays the seller a premium to obtain that right. The seller of a put undertakes the obligation to buy the stock at the strike price anytime the option is exercised before expiration. For undertaking that obligation, the seller is paid a premium.

WHAT PUTS CAN DO FOR YOU

One reason to buy a put would be owning a stock and wanting to protect yourself in the event the stock decreased in value. Suppose, for example, that you decide to purchase ABC stock at $25 a share. Obviously, if the stock went up in price, you would have the opportunity to profit. However, if the stock went down in price, you would suffer a loss. One way to protect yourself against such a loss would be to buy a put. Let us say you bought 1,000 shares of ABC for $25 a share in the middle of April. If the stock had options, you could buy a put with a strike price of $25 (or some other strike you might prefer) and you could choose any number of expirations. You would then look at option quotations to determine what premium you would have to pay in order to buy a protective put. Assume, then, that the September $25 puts could be purchased for $2.50. Since an option contract ordinarily covers a hundred shares, you could purchase 10 contracts of the September $25 puts for $2.50 a share. That would require an expenditure of $2,500 ($2.50 times 1,000 shares). Overall, you would have spent $25,000 on the stock and an additional $2,500 to buy the September $25 puts.

Now suppose that the stock dropped to $10. Had you not purchased the puts, you would have a loss of $15,000 (your original cost of $25,000 less the $10,000 to which the price fell). Since you did buy the puts, however, you could assign your stock and then force someone else to buy your stock at $25 a share even though it was trading at only $10 a share on the open market. Now, instead of losing $15 a share, you would be able to sell your stock at the same price at which you bought it and the only loss you would suffer would be the premium you paid for the puts.

AN "INSURANCE POLICY" ON YOUR STOCK: PROTECTIVE PUTS

Think of all the things you have insured. In all likelihood, you have health insurance, car insurance, homeowners or renters insurance, maybe life insurance and disability insurance. Is the jewelry insured? How about the gun collection, or the stamp collection, or whatever else precious you may have? How about your stock portfolio—is that insured?

I am struck by the vast losses suffered by many individuals and mutual funds when the bubble burst and the stock market crashed beginning in the year 2000. I have talked to many people who lost 30, 40, even 50 percent of their portfolios during that period. Most have not recovered even after the passage of several years. If we think about it, a loss of 50 percent on a stock requires the stock to move up 100 percent to get back to even. If we buy a stock at $50 a share and it drops to $25 we have lost 50 percent. Now, to get back to square one, the stock price must double. Many folks found themselves in that predicament in the most recent crash. Money intended for tuition, home ownership, or retirement simply vanished. Goals could no longer be achieved and plans had to be abandoned. As a result, a lot of people who held stock are now gun shy and do not want to risk their money in the markets. They have been burned once and do not want to risk their savings again.

Instead, what do they do? Perhaps they put their money in a savings account or a CD. The problem with those types of "investments" is that they may even guarantee a loss. If a savings account pays 3 percent annual interest and inflation is at a higher rate, the saver is doomed to lose buying power over time. The supposed safety is illusory; instead of increasing wealth, there very well could be a steady decline in the power of the money that is being saved. What a shame it is to be trapped in such a dilemma of fear. What if those people who lost so much had known a way to insure their portfolios? Would you be more likely to return to the stock market or to enter stock trading if you knew you could "insure" your positions?

The good news is that you can protect your portfolio by purchasing protective puts. As you have already seen, the purchase of a put places you in a position where you can require someone else to buy your stock at a preselected price (the strike price) for a given period of time (until the option expires). To obtain that right, you must pay a premium. The protective put, therefore, is analogous to buying an insurance policy. Just like an insurance policy, you pay a premium to obtain the protection. The expiration you choose is the equivalent of the term of the insurance policy. By choosing an at-the-money strike price, for example, you are assuring yourself that you can sell your stock at the same price for which it is currently trading during the term of the protection. In that instance, using the insurance policy analogy, you would have no deductible.

Let us look at an example. As I was writing this section, the iShares Russell 1000 Growth Index ETF (IWF) closed at precisely $55 a share. The puts with an expiration six months out were trading at $1.55 × $1.65. As you see, when option premiums are quoted, two numbers are used; the *bid* and the *ask*. The first number, the bid, is the amount someone is currently willing to pay per share (remember, one contract usually equals 100 shares) to buy the option. The second number, the ask, is the amount per share at which someone is currently willing to sell the option. In the case of the at-the-money 55 put with expiration six months away, we could have bought them for $1.65 a share. In other words, we would pay $165 per contract ($1.65 per share times 100 shares) to buy the puts. Had we chosen to buy 100 shares of IWF at $55 and "insure" it, we would have paid $5,500 for the stock and an additional $165 to buy one contract of the $55 puts. We would then have been in a position where we could have forced someone to buy our IWF stock for $55 a share ($5,500) anytime before expiration. The six-month "insurance policy" on our stock would, in effect, have no deductible. We could get exactly what we paid for it (less commissions) if we chose to exercise our put contract. The premium for the "insurance" would have been $165, so no matter how low the stock dropped during the six-month life of our put options, the worst thing that could happen would be that we would have lost the $165 in premium for the protection and whatever the commission cost would have been.

As an aside, I should mention that commissions could certainly be less than $10 or $15 a trade depending on the brokerage used. Commissions aside, we would have placed ourselves in a position where the worst scenario over the six-month term would have been a 3 percent loss ($165 premium/$5,500 cost of stock). In order to have gained the benefit of the protection in the event the stock had dropped, we would have had to take action, exercising our put and assigning the stock. We would do that by simply notifying our broker before the puts expired that we wanted to exercise them.

In the last example, the security I chose was an ETF. Since it tracks the whole Russell 1000 Growth Index, we would not expect it ever to go to zero except in some absolute national catastrophe, if then. However, had we purchased protective puts on an individual stock where the chances of dropping to nothing were much higher, we still could have assigned our stock to someone at the strike price, even if the stock no longer had any value whatsoever. Take the glaring example of Enron, a once high-flying company that crashed into bankruptcy, leaving many shareholders with stupendous losses. Had those investors simply known about buying protective puts, how different the result might have been for them.

Now we have seen a way in which to protect our stock positions so that the only amount at risk would be the premium paid for buying the protective puts. In Chapter 6, we will see how this risk can be reduced even farther—in fact, to zero or sometimes even for a guaranteed credit. In this section, we discussed "insuring" our stock with no deductible. In the next section, we will look at various decisions that can be made to reduce risk and balance the cost of protection.

CHOOSE THE TERM, PREMIUM, AND DEDUCTIBLE THAT SUITS YOU

When we buy a stock, we have a great variety of choices in how to "insure" our position. We need not simply buy a put that is in-the-money. Instead, we could choose to accept some of the risk ourselves by purchasing an out-of-the-money put, which would, of course, have a less expensive premium. We also could choose an expiration of shorter or longer duration. Obviously, the farther out the expiration, the more expensive the premium would be since the longer time would entail more time value. Table 4.4 sets out a chain of puts for Microsoft (MSFT) in mid-November at a time when the stock was trading at $29.40.

An analysis of the options chain reveals that the more time we buy (the longer the "term" or our "insurance policy"), the more expensive the option will be. We can also see that the in-the-money options are more expensive than the at-the-money options and the at-the-money options are more expensive than the out-of-the-money options.

Keeping those facts in mind, we can begin our decision-making process. If we buy the stock at $29.40, the at-the-money put (strike price closest to stock price) would be $30. If we decided we only wanted to buy "insurance" out to the nearest expiration, we would buy the December puts. If we did not want to have a deductible, we would choose the $30 strike price. As you can see from the table, the December $30 puts could be purchased for $0.75 a share. Now, we would be buying a stock at $29.40 a share and would be able to assign the stock at $30 a share anytime before the December expiration. The term of our protection would be only about a month in this case. However, the worst thing that could happen to us during that period would be that we could assign our stock at $30 a share and make

TABLE 4.4 Microsoft Chain of Put Options

Strike Price	Bid	x	Ask
December			
27.50	0	×	$0.05
30.00	$0.70	×	$0.75
32.50	$3.00	×	$3.20
January			
25.00	0	×	$0.05
27.50	$0.10	×	$0.15
30.00	$0.90	×	$1.00
32.50	$3.00	×	$3.20
April			
25.00	$0.10	×	$0.15
27.50	$0.45	×	$0.50
30.00	$1.35	×	$1.40
32.50	$3.10	×	$3.20
January (more than a year)			
25.00	$0.55	×	$0.60
27.50	$1.05	×	$1.15
30.00	$1.95	×	$2.05
35.00	$5.50	×	$5.70

$0.60 per share profit on the stock. In that circumstance, having paid $0.75 a share for the puts, we could lose no more than $0.15 a share (plus commission) overall. The at-the-money insurance policy therefore would cost us $0.75 per share for one month of protection.

Let us compare that to an "insurance policy" that would protect us for five months instead of one. If we chose to buy the April at-the-money puts, they would cost us a $1.40 per share, but that would equal only $0.28 a month in premium for the same protection.

We could also choose to buy more than a year of protection for $2.05 (expiration the following January) a share, which would equate to less than $0.16 a share per month. We should keep in mind that if we sell the stock before the puts expire, we may still be able to sell the puts as long as they have not yet expired and have some time value left. We probably would not sell the stock unless it had gone up in price, and if it had done that, the price of the puts would have declined. If the price of the stock increased enough, the puts could conceivably no longer have any value at all. However, if the stock price advanced that much, we probably would not care whether there was any value left in the puts anyway.

In each of the foregoing scenarios, I assumed that I would be buying the at-the-money puts. As you can see, in those examples, I would have purchased the stock at $29.40 and could assign the stock at $30 per share. In each instance, therefore, I would have made $0.60 per share on the sale of the stock had I exercised my puts. Suppose, however, that I was willing to take on some additional risk myself. Instead of buying at-the-money puts, I could decide to buy some out-of-the-money puts. With the stock trading at $29.40 when I bought it, I might choose to buy the $27.50 puts. If that were my decision, I could assign the stock to someone at $27.50 and would, therefore, be risking $1.90 a share ($29.40 minus $27.50) plus the cost of the protective puts. The "insurance premium" to buy the $27.50 strike price would be considerably cheaper than the premium to buy the at-the-money puts. As you can see, if I bought the April $30 puts, they would cost $1.40 a share, while the April $27.50 puts would cost only $0.50 a share. Therefore, when buying this five-month term of protection, the total risk would be $2.40 a share ($1.90 on the stock price plus $0.50 premium). In the worst case, even if the stock fell off the charts, I would have only about 8 percent risk. Theoretically, though unlikely practically, the risk of stock ownership without the protective puts would be 100 percent. By returning to her trading plan, each trader can then make a decision whether to insure any given position, and, if so, for what term, with what deductible, if any, and at what cost.

Another possibility that might be worthy of consideration would be to consider the purchase of an in-the-money put rather than an at-the-money or out-of-the-money put. In our Microsoft example, we could choose to buy the $35 puts for January the following year. If we did that, we would pay $5.70 a share (or $570 per contract) for the protection. Assume we bought the stock at $29.40, and it did not go up during the term of our option contract. Before expiration, we could assign our stock at $35 a share. Since we paid $29.40 a share and would sell it at $35 a share, we would make $5.60 a share on the sale of our stock. The puts cost $5.70. So our overall loss would be only $0.10 a share. Of course, in order for us to have profited, the stock would have had to have gone above $35.10 a share. Each of us would need to make the decision whether entry into such a position would meet our goals. If we expected a large move in the stock price, such an approach would have preserved most of our capital no matter what, and given us the opportunity to profit from a large move if one did, in fact, occur.

Another factor of which we should be cognizant is the role volatility has to play in the price of options. In the preceding discussion, I used Microsoft as an example. The stock had not been very volatile for quite some time, and for that reason the option prices were not very high. We can see a significant difference if we look at a more volatile stock. Northfield Laboratories (NFLD), for example, was quite volatile during the same period of time. On a day when the stock closed at $13.02 per share, the six-month-out expiration for the $12.50 at-the-money put was quoted at $4.30 by $5. Contrast that with the five-month-out at-the-money put for Microsoft, which was quoted at a $1.35 by $1.40.

Recognizing that the expirations for Microsoft and Northfield Laboratories are a month apart, the pricing differential between the options is, nevertheless, somewhat astonishing. The first thing to notice is that the spread between the bid and the ask price for the Microsoft at-the-money puts is only a nickel, while the spread between the bid and the ask for the at-the-money puts on Northfield Laboratories is $0.70. In the Microsoft instance, we would only have to pay $1.40 per share for an at-the-money put, while in the Northfield Laboratories case, we would be asked to pay $5 per share for the at-the-money protection. If we had to assign our Microsoft stock at $30 having purchased the five-month expiration, we would suffer a 2.7 percent loss. However, if we bought the at-the-money six-month expiration put on Northfield Laboratories for $5 and wound up assigning our stock at $12.50, we would suffer a 42.3 percent loss ($5 premium for the puts plus $0.52 loss on stock divided by $13.02).

Clearly, then, volatility plays an important role in our decision-making process. We must be aware that the premium for options on highly volatile stocks will be much higher than the premiums for options on less volatile stocks. At the same time, of course, the price movement of the more volatile stocks can be expected to be significantly greater. In each case, we have the opportunity to insure our position, but in so doing, need to be aware of the magnitude of the risks we are undertaking. In Chapter 6, I show some ways to dramatically reduce the net cost of these puts and even how to turn that cost into a credit at times.

In the examples I have given so far, I have assumed that we would pay the ask price for any options we might be buying. It definitely is worth much more than the price of this book for you to know that we may not have to pay the full ask price in every situation. Often, we can get "in between" the spread. In our Northfield Laboratories example above, the bid price was $4.30 and the ask price was $5. Here, there is a $0.70 spread between the bid price and the ask price. Instead of simply accepting and paying the $5 ask price, we could consider placing an order for less than $5. In practice, I have found that market makers will often accept a one-third reduction in the spread and sometimes even a 50 percent or greater reduction. Frequently, whether we can buy at a price below the ask and, if so, how much, will depend on how active a particular option contract is and the number of contracts the trader is attempting to purchase. In the Northfield example, I would suspect that I could probably buy the at-the-money puts for $4.80 rather than the $5 quoted. If I were buying 10 contracts, that $0.20 per share savings would equal $200—not an insignificant amount. We would try to accomplish that objective by placing a limit order to buy the options. In other words, our order would specify that we would buy at a limit of whatever price we chose and no more. If the seller were unwilling to sell at or below our limit, our order simply would not be filled, and we could modify the order or simply cancel it if we were unwilling to pay more than our limit.

The protective put strategy set out in this section is designed to protect all or a portion of our capital. In and of itself, the strategy does not result in a profit unless the stock price goes up more than the premium we paid for the protective puts. However, preservation of capital must be an important objective to any trader or investor, and this strategy is one upon which we will build as we go forward and see how we can use it in conjunction with other strategies to set up some really attractive positions.

In the next sections, we look at some other put strategies designed to produce profit with varying degrees of risk.

DIRECTIONAL PUTS

A put option may be used in a variety of ways. A person may decide to buy a put option when he believes the stock price is going down. Since the owner has the right to put his stock to someone at the strike price, the put gains value as the stock goes down in price.

Why is it that puts increase in value as the stock price drops? Let us say a stock is trading at $20 a share and we decided to buy a $22.50 put with expiration five months away. We know the put has $2.50 in intrinsic value plus some time value, perhaps $1.25, so we'll assume the total premium is $3.75. What right does the put buyer get for the $3.75 a share? He gets the right to require someone to buy his stock at the $22.50 strike price no matter how low the stock price actually goes. Assume a month goes by and the stock price has fallen to $15. Our theoretical put buyer still has the right to force someone to buy the stock at $22.50 a share even though the stock is trading at only $15 a share. Now the $22.50 put has $7.50 of intrinsic value ($22.50 minus $15) and still has four months until expiration, which means there is also some time value.

A month has passed since the put was purchased, so the time value is not as great; maybe it has been reduced to $1 from the original $1.25. So, now, the put has a value of $8.50 ($7.50 intrinsic value plus $1 time value). The put buyer in this example paid $3.75 for his put. Could he now sell the puts? Of course, and he would receive $8.50, thereby realizing a profit of $4.75 a share before commissions. That would be a return of 126 percent on the original risk. Suppose our theoretical put buyer had bought 10 contracts of those $22.50 puts at $3.75. He would have paid $3,750 (10 contracts times 100 shares per contract times $3.75 per share) plus a commission. When he sold at $8.50, he would have received $8,500 (10 contracts times 100 shares per contract times $8.50 per contract) less a commission. Do trades like that occur in real life? Absolutely. Did the put buyer in the example have to own any stock? No, he could have first bought and then later sold his put contracts. He would have simply traded a directional put. The put buyer may not own any stock at all, but only seek to profit as the value of his put goes up when the price of the stock goes down. At some point, he will simply sell the put he had bought. The trader who believes that a stock price is going to go down could then buy a directional put with the intention of selling it later at a profit if his prediction that the stock price was going to drop was correct.

An example of a trade I actually made was the purchase of five contracts of the May $80 puts on Whole Food Markets, Inc. (WFMI). I entered the position on January 12 and paid $7.80 for these puts that were then about $4.00 in-the-money with the stock trading around $76. My total cost to enter the position was $3,900 (5 contracts times 100 shares per contract times $7.80 per share) plus a small commission. The stock price dropped fairly quickly, adding value to my position. Five days later, on January 17, after I bought the puts, the stock was trading near $73 a share and my puts had increased in value to $9.50. I closed the position by selling the five contracts at $9.50 and took in $4,750 less a small commission. Before commissions, then, I realized a gain of $850 or a return on risk of 21.8 percent in only five days! As you can see, I opened the position by buying in-the-money puts about four full months from expiration.

This strategy of buying a directional put is similar to selling a stock short, but, unlike selling a stock short, where the risk is theoretically unlimited, the risk in buying the put is limited to the price of the put. In the previous example of my trade on the WFMI puts, the most I could have lost would have been the $7.80 premium I paid to enter the position. Even that would be very unlikely since the stock would have had to have gone up fairly dramatically in price while I did nothing. Had the stock moved against me, I would have had the chance to sell my position to close it out before I lost my whole investment. Since I had purchased the $80 puts when they were about $4 in-the-money (with the stock trading near $76), those puts would still have had a value around $4 even if the stock stayed the same price until expiration. In other words, with the stock at $76 just before expiration and if I still owned the $80 puts, they would have an intrinsic value of $4, and I could sell them for that, losing only about $3.80 a share. The fact is that I would undoubtedly have exited the position long before expiration if the stock started to move up or even if the price began to stagnate.

When we buy directional puts, we want the stock price to go down. The only way we make money buying directional puts is if the stock drops in price and does so relatively quickly (and/or sometimes if volatility increases). If we buy a directional put, we probably will not profit if the stock price stays the same or if the stock price goes up.

One of the drawbacks of buying options is that they expire. Another drawback is that the time value portion of the option premium decreases as time elapses, and the closer to expiration, the faster the time value dissipates. For those reasons, when I am buying options, particularly for a directional play such as the strategy I just discussed, I like to buy a lot of time. Generally speaking, when buying directional put options, I prefer to buy an expiration that is at least five or six months away. Farther out expirations, as we have seen, are more expensive, but in the beginning the time value does not vanish as quickly. I also prefer to buy options that are one or two strikes in-the-money. As we have seen, time value is most expensive in the at-the-money options, so when I buy in-the-money options, I am not paying as much for time as I would if I were buying the at-the-money strikes. Since the in-the-money options have some intrinsic value, they also usually have a higher delta. Delta is a measurement of how much an option price is expected to move with each dollar the stock price moves. (Since we are talking about puts in this chapter, I should note that the delta of puts is written with a minus sign). A put with delta of -0.60, for example, suggests the option price will move 60 cents for every dollar the stock price moves up or down. If I buy an option with a higher delta and I am right on the direction of the stock movement, I'll profit more quickly. The opposite is also true. If I am wrong on the direction, the value of my option will decrease more quickly with a higher delta.

If I had to choose between buying in-the-money options with a high delta or buying more time, I would probably opt for more time. But if cost is the consideration, I would still like to buy longer-term in-the-money options for directional positions and would, perhaps, buy fewer contracts.

SELLING NAKED PUTS

It can be a lot of fun to go naked as long as we understand and appreciate the risks. Selling naked puts *under the right conditions* is one of my favorite income-producing strategies. Brokers will often tell you that selling naked puts is a risky strategy, but the question is: To whom is it most risky? The fact is—and I'll discuss this shortly—that selling naked puts is less risky than simply buying a stock. First, though, let's define the strategy of selling naked puts. You already know what a put is, and you are familiar with the concept of selling. *Naked* simply means that you own no underlying stock. When a trader sells naked puts, he collects a premium in exchange for undertaking the obligation to buy the stock at the strike price if it is assigned to him at any time before expiration. In effect, the trader becomes the "insurance company." He receives a premium for taking the risk that the stock can be assigned to him at the strike price anytime before the put contract expires. Who makes more money than the insurance companies?

Suppose in late November you liked XYZ stock at $35 a share, and assume that the December $35 puts are quoted at a $1.50 by $1.75. You could decide to sell one contract of those December $35 puts and would receive $150 in your account the following day less the commission. Under that circumstance, the market has paid you $150 to buy XYZ stock for the same $35 a share you were already willing to pay. If the stock is below $35 a share at expiration, it will be assigned to you at $35 a share. What, then, is your actual cost in the stock? The market has already paid you $1.50 a share so your net cost before commissions is only $33.50 a share. Now, tell me, which is riskier, buying XYZ stock at $35 a share or buying XYZ stock at $33.50 a share? Had you bought the stock at $35 a share, your risk would have been $35 a share. However, had you sold the $35 puts for $1.50 a share your risk would only be $33.50 a share.

Though it is clear that the risk is less if the market has paid you a premium to buy the stock than it would be had you just bought the stock without receiving a premium, your broker considers this strategy to be quite risky. In fact, in order to sell naked puts, most brokerages require that you have some minimum amount of money in your account, experience trading options, and that you are a Level 4 trader. If you ultimately decide that you would like to sell naked puts, it is imperative that you check with your broker to determine the minimum account balance required by it to sell naked puts. Some brokerages demand account balances as high as $100,000 or more, while others may require only $2,000 or $5,000.

Brokerage clients are classified by specific trading levels. One broker with which I am familiar uses the following classifications:

Level 0: Buy stocks, bonds, and/or mutual funds.

Level 1: Covered calls and selling stock short.

Level 2: Buying calls and puts.

Level 3: Debit spreads (purchasing spreads).

Level 4: Credit spreads and selling naked puts.

Level 5: Selling naked calls and selling naked options on indexes.

Each brokerage makes its own determination as to an individual trader's assigned level. The determination is based, among other things, on the trader's representation of his own trading experience. Though I am definitely not suggesting this approach, a trader could open an account and lie on his application by stating that he has several years' option trading experience when, in fact, he may have no such experience at all. That person could very well be assigned Level 4, though, in reality, he was completely inexperienced. Obviously, it would be extraordinarily foolish to make such a misrepresentation. However, it illustrates who is really being protected by the level assignment. Certainly, it is not the trader. It is the brokerage firm. Should the trader later make a claim against the brokerage that he should not have been permitted to engage in a strategy such as selling naked puts because he did not know what he was doing, the brokerage can quite probably successfully defend itself on the ground that the trader had represented himself to be experienced.

Why is it that brokerages are so wary about permitting customers to engage in the selling naked puts strategy? The fact is that many brokerages permit even a Level 1 trader to write covered calls, yet they require a trader to be Level 4 to sell naked puts. As you will see, the risk graph for writing covered calls is precisely the same as the risk graph for selling naked puts. The apparent inconsistency has a historical basis. Prior to the crash of 1987, selling naked puts became a very popular and prevalent strategy. Many traders were mindlessly selling naked puts to generate regular income without regard to risk. Often, these traders were working from margin accounts. A margin account is one in which the trader is enabled to borrow from the broker. When the crash of 1987 occurred, stock was put to many of the traders who were unable to pay for it because they were on margin. As a result, some brokerages took terrible hits. I believe that the risk the brokers now perceive is more to them than it is to their clients. Quite understandably, the brokers have learned an expensive lesson that they do not care to repeat. They are, therefore, extremely cautious in permitting any individual trader to sell naked puts and will, if given the opportunity, discourage the use of that strategy.

Having said all that, under the right circumstances, I really like the selling naked put strategy. When using this strategy, as with all strategies, it is imperative that the trader understand precisely what he is doing and what risk he is undertaking. First, it is essential to understand that selling naked puts is a very bullish strategy. If it is to be undertaken at all, I would suggest that it be applied only during an uptrending market or to an uptrending sector and to an uptrending stock. In this strategy, I am selling to open the position. Therefore, a credit is coming into my account the following day. I have invested nothing, but the market is paying me to undertake some risk.

Ultimately, the question for me becomes what risk I am going to assume. Unlike the situation where I am buying options, when selling an option like a naked put, I much prefer to sell a short amount of time, and I sell out-of-the-money options. When the options are out-of-the-money, the premium consists completely of time value, so the only thing I am selling is time. Remember, the closer to expiration, the faster the time value runs out. My goals, then, when selling naked puts are to sell nothing but time and to sell only a relatively short amount of time. When I do that, the premium can disappear rapidly. I then have a couple of choices: I can wait until expiration and keep the whole premium I originally received if the stock price has not dropped below the strike I sold, or I can close the position early by "buying back" the puts I sold. I do not necessarily have to wait until expiration to close the position, if time value has decreased, I can buy to close the position and keep the difference between what I sold the puts for and what it cost to buy them back.

A couple of real-life examples illustrate how a naked put trade can work. On May 23, Phelps Dodge (PD) gapped up at the open and traded between $83.03 and $86.99. June option expiration was 24 days away. I was able to open a small position, selling only three contracts of the June 80 puts for $2.15 and, before commission, took in $645 (3 contracts times 100 shares per contract times $2.15). That cash was in my account the following day. After moving up over the course of a few days, the stock plunged on June 5, trading as low as $82.95. I decided to close my position and bought to close the June 80 puts for $1.15, paying $345 before commissions. As you can see, since I sold the 80 puts out-of-the-money when the stock was trading above $83, the total premium I collected was for time. After 12 days, the stock was trading near the same price as when I sold my puts, but, due to the passage of time, the premium had dropped 95 cents a share. Now, I was able to buy back what I had sold at $2.15 for only $1.15 and pocket the difference (after commission) as my profit. That was a $300 gain before commission in just 12 days! What had I invested? I had no investment—none. The market literally paid me $300 to take on an obligation for only 12 days. The only requirement was that I have some money on hold during the period of my trade, which will be discussed a little later. While $300 may not seem like a lot of money, an additional $300 a week or a month or in 12 days can make an important difference in the lives of many and, in any event, would buy an awfully good dinner.

Here is another example. On June 30, Investment Technology (ITG) broke out above a little area of consolidation and traded between $47.47 and $50.86. July expiration was three weeks away. This time, I sold just five contracts of the July $45 puts for $0.85 and, before commission, brought in $425. As you can see, I was in no danger of having the stock put (assigned) to me unless it fell below $45 a share. It closed that day at $50.86, so it would have to fall almost $6 before I would have to worry about having it put to me. On July 10, after the passage of 10 days, the stock had a down day and traded between $48.33 and $49.73, still far away from any danger zone. However, time had passed and I did not like how the stock was behaving, so I decided to close my position. Remember, I had sold my July $45 puts for $0.85. Even though the stock was trading in roughly the same area it had been when I sold my puts, the premium for the July $45 puts had dropped to just $0.40 when I bought them back (bought to close the position). In this instance, I enjoyed a gain of $0.45 a share or $225 in just 10 days before the commissions.

I am sure you have noticed that whenever I speak of gains or losses in trades, I have noted that they are before commissions. Since individual brokerages charge different commissions, I leave out that part of the ultimate profit or loss calculation. One trader may be paying $12.95 for one side of an option trade, while another may pay double that or more. The important point to consider is that commissions do factor into how much a trader actually does make or lose on a trade. I urge you to be mindful of the effect commissions have on your trading profitability. Later in the book, I devote a little time to discussing brokers, brokerages, and commissions. In that section, I try to point out reasons why it may sometimes be smart to pay higher commissions and other instances where heavily discounted commissions might be the better choice.

In the section on buying protective puts, I used Northfield (NFLD) as an example of a stock that was then volatile and had fairly expensive options as a consequence. I prefer to buy options that are cheap and sell ones that are expensive, so when I saw the NFLD situation, I decided to see what I might be able to do selling some naked puts. Table 4.5 shows the option chain for the December puts, with NFLD stock trading at $15.43 on November 24.

Expiration is 21 days away. Let us assume that we have decided to sell 10 naked put contracts and we want to choose which strike to sell. The $15 puts are only slightly out-of-the-money, and we know this stock is fairly volatile, so there is a pretty good chance that the stock will drop below $15

TABLE 4.5   December Expiration—NFLD Puts

Strike	Bid	x	Ask
7.50	$0.50	×	$0.55
10.00	$0.80	×	$0.95
12.50	$1.30	×	$1.40
15.00	$2.25	×	$2.40
17.50	$3.60	×	$4.10

and we would have a relatively high risk of having the stock assigned to us at $15. If we look at the chart below, we can see that there is a support level around $14 and a trend support about $13. If we chose to sell the $12.50 puts, the stock would have to break both of those supports within the next three weeks to put us in any danger of assignment. Of course, if it broke either or both of those supports, we could immediately buy to close our position and, depending on how much time elapsed before the supports were broken, could either make a bit of gain or suffer a fairly small loss. If we did decide to sell the December 12.50 puts, we know we could get $1.30 a share or $1,300 for the 10 contracts.

In looking at Table 4.5, I saw that there was yet another support in the $12 area, so I decided to sell the $10 December puts for $0.80 and took in $800. Now, I don't have to worry about assignment unless the stock price drops more than $5.43 and through three levels of support. If it does drop through the second level of support, I'll look to exit my position, and if some time has passed, I'll probably be able to keep some of the $800 I received in premium. Of course, if the stock stays above $10 until expiration, I keep the whole $800 less the commission.

As you can see in Figure 4.1, the strike I actually chose was below at least three levels of support, so selling the $10 puts three weeks from expiration looks like a pretty conservative play. Even with high volatility, it does not look like there is a high likelihood of the price dropping below $10. Of course, I could have opted to take in more money at the outset by selling the $12.50 puts for $1.30, but I like my odds better at the $10 strike. Now, even if the stock dropped and were put to me at $10, my net cost would be only $9.20 since the market gave me $0.80 in the first place.

FIGURE 4.1 NFLD Chart Illustrating Support Levels. (Telechart 2005® chart courtesy of Worden Brothers, Inc.)

You may recall that when I discussed buying a directional put, I mentioned that the stock must move down for me to make money. If the stock price stays the same or goes up when I own (or am long) a directional put, I will lose. Now consider the situation with selling a naked put. In the NFLD example, I sold a $10 put for $0.80 and was paid that amount right away. If the stock goes up from the current $15.43, no one would put it to me at $10, so I would keep the $0.80; if the stock stays the same, no one would put it to me at $10, so I would keep the $0.80; even if the stock went down more than $5, as long as it did not go below about $10, no one would put it to me. So, here, I profit if the stock goes up, if it stays the same, and even if it goes down, in this case as much as $5. Instead of a one-in-three chance to profit as in the case of buying a directional put, I have at least a two out of three chance to profit, and may even have a three out of three chance to profit if the stock moves slightly against me when I sell a naked put. The risk when buying the directional put is limited to the price paid for the put. The risk in selling the naked put is that the stock could be assigned to me and I would have to buy the stock.

In the NFLD example, I would have to pay $10 a share for the stock (less the $0.80 the market paid me to take the risk), and the stock could then theoretically drop to zero. When we analyze these strategies, we must do so in light of our own situation. We should go back to our own business plan, hearken to our own risk tolerance, and see what reward-to-risk ratio lies within our personal comfort zone.

As I mentioned earlier, this strategy brings in cash with nothing invested. However, you do need to be aware that some assets in your account will be on "hold" while you have any open naked put positions. That amount is calculated daily by your broker, so it is "marked to market." The calculation to determine the amount on "hold" is as follows:

> 25 percent of the underlying market price
> + the premium
> − the amount out of the money

or

> 10 percent of the underlying market price (or strike price
> for out of the money puts)
> + the premium

whichever is greater.

Let us assume we open a position by selling 10 contracts of the at-the-money $30 puts on DEF stock that is trading at $30 and that we receive a premium of $2. How much would be on hold in our account? The value of the underlying would be $30,000 (10 contracts times 100 shares per contract times $30 a share), so 25 percent of that would be $7,500. We received $2,000 in premium (10 contracts times 100 shares per contract times $2 per share premium) so we would add that to the $7,500 and the result is $9,500, since there is no amount out-of-the-money in this example. Ten percent of the market price of the underlying is only $3,000, and, obviously, $9,500 is greater, so we would have $9,500 on hold.

If we look at my NFLD trade, the stock was trading at $15.43 and I entered the position by selling 10 contracts of the $10 puts and received a premium of $0.80. The calculation there would be 25 percent of the underlying (1,000 shares times $15.43 times 25 percent) equals $3,857.50 plus the premium ($800) equals $4,657.50 minus the amount out-of-the-money ($5.43 times 1,000 shares equals $5,430) equals −$772.50. Naturally, the broker is not going to give me a credit in this situation, so I need to do the alternate calculation of 10 percent of the underlying ($15.43 price per share times 1,000 shares times 10 percent), which equals $1,543 plus the premium of $800, which equals $2,343. Since $2,343 is greater than −$772.50, the amount on hold would be $2,343.

While it certainly cannot hurt to know the formula to calculate the amount on hold, there are a couple of other, much easier ways to see how much is going to be on hold. First, the amount on hold is roughly 30 percent of the underlying, so you can get a ballpark number that way. The other way is to simply contact your broker. Some brokerage web sites do the calculation automatically for you.

LOW-RISK TRADES

As I mentioned, selling naked puts is one of my favorite strategies under the right circumstances, but I have Level 5 trader status. Your broker may not be willing to grant you even Level 4 until you have more experience and may require a higher minimum in your account than you are willing or able to provide. As with any strategy, you should practice selling naked puts before using real money. Some brokers' web sites actually have "virtual trading" features that enable you to practice without putting your real cash at risk. Whether you do or do not decide that trading naked puts is a strategy for you, there is another strategy using puts that is worth exploring.

This strategy combines high monthly returns with limited risk. It is the credit spread using puts. A spread is a position involving two or more legs. In the first example, we will look at the bullish put spread. Bullish suggests that the market, sector, and/or stock are going up in price, so when we use a bullish put spread, we want to take advantage of that upward movement. The bullish put spread is similar to selling naked puts in that we will be selling a put and will receive cash into our account the next business day. It differs from the naked put sale in the amount of credit received and in the size of the risk that is undertaken. As you may recall, the risk in a naked put sale is that the stock will actually be assigned to us at the strike price we sold, and when we own the stock, the risk is the price of the stock. If we sold 10 contracts of the $50 strike puts on XYZ and it was assigned to us at $50, we would have the whole $50,000 at risk because theoretically, at least, the stock price could go to zero. If we create a spread, however, our risk will be significantly reduced.

Using the XYZ example above, assume the stock is trading just above a support level and the current stock price is $51. We could get $2.50 by selling the $50 naked put, but our risk would be the price of the stock if it were assigned to us. Assume we do sell 10 contracts of the $50 puts and take in the $2,500, but at the same time let us also buy 10 contracts of the $45 puts with the same expiration for $1.50 or a total of $1,500. As you can see, we are taking in $2,500 and paying out $1,500 so there will be a net credit of $1,000 going into our account. We are receiving $1,000 more than we are paying and we now have a two-legged (or spread) position. We have sold the 50 puts, which means we have taken on the obligation to buy the stock at $50 a share ($50,000 for the 10 contracts), but we also bought the $45 puts. Buying the $45 puts gives us the right to assign the stock to someone else at 45 a share ($45,000 for the 10 contracts), so in the worst case scenario, if we were forced to buy the 1,000 shares of XYZ at $50,000, we could immediately turn around and force someone else to buy the stock from us for $45,000. Yes, we would suffer a $5,000 loss, but is that a better risk than the naked put where the stock could be put to us for $50,000 and we are at the mercy of the market price? What if the stock had dropped to $30 a share? If we were in the spread, it would not matter, we could still exercise our $45 puts and sell the stock for $45,000; the loss would be $5,000. However, if we had just sold the naked puts and the stock was put to us, our loss would be $20,000.

Clearly, by entering the spread, we have reduced our risk. But with the spread, is our risk really $5,000? No, it is not. Remember, the market paid us $1,000 when we entered the spread and we are able to keep that money so the risk is really only $4,000; the $5,000 spread less the credit we received at entry. Look at the return on risk in our example. We are risking $4,000 and have received a return of $1,000. The potential return on risk is 25 percent ($1,000 return divided by $4,000 risk)! We can often find that kind of return for a month! Of course, we also took in a smaller credit by choosing the spread over the naked put sale, but we greatly reduced the risk and have a hefty return on the risk we are taking.

One other important factor is that we do not need to be a Level 4 trader to enter spread positions. We can enter spreads as a Level 3 trader and Level 3 is much, much easier to attain. If you look at the example trade from the broker's point of view, the spread puts only $4,000 at risk and that full amount is on hold while the naked put trade puts $50,000 less the premium received at risk and has only about $15,000 (roughly 30 percent of the underlying) on hold.

In my experience, it is not too hard to find bullish put credit spreads that offer a potential 20 to 30 percent return on risk per month! Even with only three weeks remaining before expiration, it is not unusual to find returns on risk that are greater than 15 percent. Take a look at the put option chain I set out on NFLD in the naked put section. Remember, the stock was trading at $15.43 and there was a support at $14. If I decided to sell the first strike below support, I could sell the December $12.50 puts for $1.30 (quoted at $1.30 × $1.40). Exactly three weeks remained until expiration. If I were doing a 10-contract spread, I would take in $1,300. At the same time, to create the spread, I could buy the $10 puts for $0.95 and pay $950. (In fact, I could probably buy the $10 puts for $0.90 instead of $0.95 since the spread on the bid × ask is $0.80 × $0.95 and I can usually get one third off the spread). If I take in $1,300 and pay out $950, I will have a net credit of $350 coming into my account. Initially, my risk would be $2,500 because the stock could be assigned to me at $12.50 ($12,500) and I could, in turn, assign it to someone else for $10 ($10,000); but, here again, the market paid me a credit of $350 to enter the position, so my risk is $2,500 minus the $350 or an actual risk of $2,150. The return on risk, therefore, is potentially 16.3 percent ($350 divided by $2,150) for just three weeks. If I were able to buy the $10 puts for $0.90, as I feel confident I could, I would then take in a credit of $400 instead of $350 and the risk would only be $2,100, so the return on risk potentially would be 19 percent ($400 divided by $2,100). Sixteen percent or 19 percent in three weeks certainly is not a bad return when we realize that is four or five times what a CD might pay in a whole year.

I like credit spreads, and I am particularly fond of those where the strike prices are only $2.50 apart. Even better are the stocks that offer strikes that are only $1 apart because the dollar risk is even lower. Take a stock like Oracle (ORCL), for example, that has $1 strikes as of the time of this writing. The stock is trading at $19.60 and support is above $19. The three-week-out December 19 put option is quoted at $0.20 × $0.25, so if I were to sell 20 contracts, I could take in $400. The December $18 strike is trading at $0.05 × $0.10, so if I bought 20 contracts it would cost me $200. Creating the December $19/$18 bullish put spread would bring in a net of $200. The risk would be $1,800 so the return on risk would potentially be 11 percent for three weeks.

I once had a student in one of my seminars raise his hand and tell me he did not like a trade where I only made a dime on a dollar spread. He turned his nose up at the dime. The fact is that a dime on a dollar spread is a return on risk of 11 percent ($0.10 cash in divided by $0.90 risk). I asked him what annual return he was making and he said around 8 percent—8 percent *annually* and he was criticizing 11 percent a month—go figure! I agree that 10 cents is not very much, but I know 11 percent per month is more than most are making. If I am going to enter spread positions on stocks with $1 spreads where I am making only a dime, I must consider a couple of factors very seriously. I need to be sure I am entering a large enough position that I overcome the effect of commissions, and I need to be sure there is enough *open interest* to permit me to enter a position with a fairly large number of existing contracts.

Open interest is the number of contracts actually existing on a given option contract. Open interest should not be confused with volume, which is the number of contracts traded in a day. Let me suggest—no, let me urge—that you always check open interest. If the open interest is low, it may be very difficult to get out of a position without getting burned since there may not be enough liquidity. My rule of thumb in trading option contracts (except for buying protective puts) is that I want open interest to exceed 300 contracts and, unless I am buying protective puts, I never want to own more than 5 to 7 percent of the open interest. If the open interest is 400, I would not consider holding more than about 20 contracts.

In the Oracle example where the trader could make $0.10 a share or an 11 percent return on risk, the open interest on the December $19 puts was 12,143 contracts and the open interest on the December 18s was 8,523. In my example, I chose a 20 contract, a leg position, which was well within my guidelines. A 40 or even 50 contract, a side position, would fit my parameters for open interest. If the trader chose 50 contracts, he would bring in $500 and have $4,500 at risk. It still works out to a potential return on risk of 11 percent for three weeks. The important point is what percentage return you are achieving, not whether you are achieving it with dimes or with dollars. If I have $10,000 and can make $1,100 a month with it, do I care whether it comes in $5, $1, $0.25, or even $0.10 increments? No, the idea is to make the return.

As I said earlier, I find many spreads each month that offer potential returns on risk of up to 35 percent per month. Most seem to fall in the 20 to 30 percent range, and, to my mind, that is not bad.

When I wrote about what strike price to select when selling a naked put, I suggested that an out-of-the-money strike below a support be chosen. The same holds true of the short leg (the leg you are selling) of a bullish put spread. I sell an out-of-the-money strike below a support and I normally buy the next strike below to create my spread. In other words, if the strikes are $2.50 apart and I am selling the $17.50 strike, I will ordinarily buy the $15 strike. I could choose to buy a lower strike, like the $12.50 or the $10 as my long or protective leg (the leg I am buying), and that would bring in more cash, but it would also increase the risk.

The type of spread we have been reviewing is a vertical spread and, in case it is not obvious, I am selling and buying different strike puts, but with the same expiration. I also enter both legs at the same time. As noted earlier, when I am selling options, I like to sell time value only and relatively short amounts of time. Since the bullish put credit spreads bring cash in, they are net sales. I sell the out-of-the-money put because the premium is comprised of nothing but time value, and I sell a short amount of time since the shorter the life remaining in the option, the faster the time value runs out.

If I have entered a bullish put spread, my job is to keep the credit I got. Suppose I sold the $20 strike and bought the $17.50 strike for a credit of $0.50. As long as the stock stays above $20 until expiration, I have nothing to worry about. No one would assign the stock to me at $20 if it could be sold for more than that on the open market. If it stays above $20 until expiration, I just keep what I got when I entered the position and go on about my business. What happens if the stock falls below the strike price of my short position (the strike price of the leg I sold)? Now I am at risk of having the stock assigned to me and taking a loss. I have several alternatives. If there is a lot of time left and it looks like the stock might go back up, I can do nothing and see what happens. If there is not much time left until expiration, and I have no specific reason to believe the stock might bounce up quickly, I could unwind my whole position. That is, I could buy to close the leg I originally sold to open and I could sell to close the leg I originally bought to open. In that instance, I would likely reduce my loss below the maximum and be out of the whole position. If there were a lot of time left and it looked like the stock might continue to fall, I could buy to close my short leg (the one I sold to open) and hold on to the protective leg (the one I bought to open). As the price of the stock falls, the long or protective leg should gain in value, particularly if there is a fair amount of time left. I could wait to sell the long leg until the whole position became profitable.

On occasion, I have done exactly that and made more than I would have if the stock had stayed above the original short leg strike price. Be aware, however, that there is danger in the latter approach. When we entered the spread in the first place, there was a predefined risk, that is, the spread minus the credit received. Once the short leg is closed, the risk can increase; the value of the remaining leg can go to zero if the stock price turns back up. In this case, we are trying to reduce loss and even, perhaps, turn a loss into a gain if the value of the long remaining leg goes up, but we are also increasing risk. Unless there is quite a bit of time left, I prefer to close out the whole position and take whatever lumps I must. Sometimes, if there is a lot of time left (like three weeks when I started the spread a month before expiration), I may hold the long leg until the downward price move begins to slacken and then I close that leg as well.

SUMMARY

This chapter covered several uses of the put option. We have seen how to use puts to "insure" or hedge a position; we have seen how to use puts to make money in a directional move; and we have looked at a couple of ways to make income using naked puts or bullish put spreads. I have tried to explain the risks of each of these strategies and you should be sure you understand the risks before using real money in the trades. You can make a lot of money using these strategies, but do not let greed push you into taking risks before you have practiced each strategy without real money.

The put strategies I covered here are some of my favorites, and some that have been very successful for me. You should be aware that there are many other strategies available using puts, but if you learn what I have set out here, you will be well on your way to improving your trading. In the next chapter, I take a look at call options and, after that, put together some combinations of puts and calls that can result in some highly profitable and extremely low-risk (sometimes even no-risk) trades.

CHAPTER 5

How Call Options Can Really Make You Rich

I n Chapter 4, we discussed put options in great detail. Now it's time to take an in-depth look at call options and what they can do for us. To review, an option is a contract under which the buyer obtains rights and the seller undertakes obligations. The call option is a contract in which the buyer obtains the right, but does not have the obligation, to buy the stock at the strike price any time before expiration. For that right, the buyer pays the seller a premium. In exchange for the premium, the seller of a call option undertakes the obligation to deliver the stock at the strike price any time before expiration if "called" (assigned).

Just as with the case of the put options, call options are traded by contract and, ordinarily, a contract controls 100 shares of stock. Always remember to check to be sure the contract you are looking at is one that does control 100 shares of stock. Occasionally, a contract may control a number other than 100 shares as the result of a split or some other activity related to the stock. Just as in the case of put options, call option contracts also expire at market close on the third Friday of the month. Remember, technically, option contracts expire at noon on the Saturday following the third Friday of the month, but since we retail traders cannot trade on Saturdays, the effective expiration for us is at the market close on the third Friday.

Again, as in the case of put options, most call options on equities (stocks) are American style and may be exercised any time before expiration. While both American-style puts and American-style calls may be exercised at any time before expiration, my experience has taught me that a put option is more likely to be exercised early than is a call option. I have found that it is much more common to exercise calls at, rather than very much before, expiration.

In this chapter, we will look at a variety of strategies that utilize calls. We will see how to use calls as a purely directional strategy to profit when a stock moves up in price. As part of that directional strategy, we also will explore the use of long-term calls or LEAPS®. Calls can also be used to reduce risk when stock is sold short. We can generate regular income by selling (writing) covered calls against stock positions we own, and we can even sell them to bring in cash as we create spreads with other call options we own.

DIRECTIONAL CALLS

Call options, like put options, may be used in a variety of ways. One of the most common reasons to purchase a call option is an attempt to profit from an upward move in the stock price. Since the owner of a call option has the right to buy the stock at the strike price any time before expiration, the call option gains in value as the stock price increases. Let us take a look at why calls gain value as stock prices increase.

Suppose a stock is trading at $26 a share and we decide to buy a $25 call with expiration six months away. When we buy the $25 call, we have obtained the right to buy the stock at $25 a share at any time until expiration. If the stock is already trading at $26, there is $1 of intrinsic value, and since six months remain to expiration, we know there is going to be some time value. If the time value is another $1, the total premium would be $2 per share, so for each contract (controlling 100 shares), we would pay $200 plus commission. Let us assume that six weeks pass and the stock price has jumped to $30 a share. We still have the right to buy the stock at $25 a share, so now the intrinsic value of our call option is $5 and there are still four and a half months until the contract expires, so there is still time value. Time has passed, so the time value is probably less than when we bought the calls. Suppose the time value is now $0.60. We paid $2 for the calls, and now they are worth $5.60 ($5 intrinsic plus $0.60 time value). We could sell the options for $5.60 and realize a $3.60 a share gain. We invested $2 and would have made a $3.60 profit for a gain of 180 percent. The potential leverage is phenomenal.

Compare that to the situation that would have existed had we bought the stock instead of the call options. We would have paid $26 a share and achieved a profit of $4 a share for a return of 15 percent. While 15 percent would not be anything to sneeze at, it does not approach the 180 percent gain that would be possible with the calls. Notice that we would have made a much greater percentage gain using the calls, while we would have had a higher dollar-per-share gain if we had bought the stock instead. Our investment if we had bought 100 shares of the stock at $26 would have been $2,600, while it would have been only $200 if we bought the calls. What about the risk? If we bought the stock, theoretically at least, the price could go to zero, so we could lose $2,600. If we bought the calls, our loss would be limited to the price we paid for the calls or $200.

Those calls sound awfully good, don't they? Remember, though, that options expire. Suppose the stock did not move up in price over the six-month life of our options. If it stayed at $26 at expiration and we owned the stock, we would have lost nothing and would still own the stock. However, if we had bought the $25 calls, there would be no time value at expiration, and there would be only $1 intrinsic value just before expiration, so we would have to sell them and lose a dollar of our original $2 investment. If we did not do something before expiration like sell our calls or exercise them, we would lose the whole value since once they expire they are gone.

As we saw with put options, when we buy an option (whether put or call) in an effort to profit from a directional move in the stock, we will profit only if the stock moves in the right direction (and fairly promptly). We will lose if the stock price stays the same or moves in the direction opposite the direction we want it to go. If we buy a call, in order for us to make money, the stock must go up. If the price stays the same or goes down, we will suffer a loss.

The strategy of buying call options is similar to buying stock, but when buying call options, we can control the same number of shares at a much lesser cost than if we bought the stock. If the stock does move in our favor, calls will provide a much greater percentage return, while stock ownership will ordinarily provide a greater dollar return. Stock ownership also presents a much higher dollar risk than call ownership (assuming the same number of shares controlled), but call ownership runs the risk that time will run out and the options expire before a profit can be realized.

LEAPS®

Long-term equity anticipation securities (LEAPS) are one of my favorite ways to trade calls. In Chapter 4, I discussed my preference for selling short-term out-of-the-money options. The opposite is true when I am buying options. When buying options, I like to buy a great deal of time and I prefer to buy in-the-money options. LEAPS were developed by the Chicago Board Options Exchange and the name is a registered trademark. They have expirations up to three years out and essentially trade as options.

When buying such a far-out expiration, it does not mean that I intend to hold the position until expiration. Many times, I may hold them for only a relatively short time. For example, on November 14, 2006, with the stock trading around $52 a share, I bought five contracts of the January 2008 $50 LEAPS calls on Armor Holdings (AH) for $9.70. The cost, including a commission of $12.95 was $4,862.95. Two days later, I sold my calls for $10.10. After commission, I took in $5,036. 89. After paying the commissions, I realized a return of 3.6 percent. A 1.8 percent per day gain is definitely acceptable in my book!

In another instance, in the latter part of July 2006, with Oracle (ORCL) trading near $15 a share, I bought the January 2008 $12.50 LEAPS calls for $4.20 a share. This time, I held the position for about two months and sold my calls for $6.20 a share. I made $2 on a $4.20 investment. Before commission, that equaled a 47.6 percent return on my investment or a little better than 23 percent per month. Again, while we always need to be aware of the effect of commissions, that cost was of very little consequence in these trades.

On August 15, 2006, I bought five contracts of the January 2008 LEAPS calls on Qualcomm (QCOM), a stock whose options I have played many times. They cost me $9.30, or a total of $4,662.95 including commission. The stock was then trading at $34.86. The next morning, the stock gapped up $0.83 on the open and I sold part of my position (three of my five contracts) for $10.40 and a $1.10 a share profit on those contracts. That was an 11.8 percent gain on the option price overnight! I held on to two of the contracts for two more days, and then sold them for $10.60, up $1.30 from my entry. That was a 13.9 percent gain on those two contracts in just three days. After commissions, I made $550 in three days.

There are a number of reasons why I like LEAPS when I am entering a directional call position. First, they provide a lot of time for the stock to move up, and, if I am going to make money on a directional call position, the stock must go up in price. Second, when buying a LEAPS call, the time value is cheaper per unit than the time value for a shorter-term call. As I write this section, Home Depot (HD) is trading for a little under $40 a share, so the $40 strike price premium is all time value. The premium for the $40 May 2007 expiration (five and a half months away) is $2.40, or about $0.44 a month. The premium for a $40 LEAPS call with an expiration in January 2009 (24 and a half months away) is $5.30, so the time value is only about $0.22 a month. In other words, on a per-unit-of-time basis in the Home Depot example, we would pay almost twice as much per month in time value to buy the shorter-term call than we would to buy the LEAPS call. In general, the more time we buy, the less the cost per unit of time, although the overall cost is usually greater. A third reason for buying a lot of time is that the time value does not erode as quickly in an option with more time to expiration as it does in an option that is closer to expiration. Also, when buying a LEAPS call, the delta is generally higher than the delta of a shorter-term call with the same strike price.

As I mentioned earlier, when buying options, I not only like to buy a lot of time, but also, I usually buy in-the-money, options since they already have intrinsic value and have a higher delta than at-the-money or out-of-the-money options. Remember, delta is a measure of how much the option price is expected to move when the stock price moves $1. If the delta is 0.50, for example, the option price would be expected to move $0.50 for each $1 the stock moves. Looking at the same strike price, we normally see that the delta of a LEAPS call is greater than the delta of the same strike option with an earlier expiration. In the Home Depot $40 strike discussed above, the expiration five and a half months out was May and the delta as of the time of this writing was 0.52, suggesting for each dollar the stock moved, the option would move $0.52. However, the delta of the $40 LEAPS call with a January 2009 expiration (24 and a half months away) was 0.62, suggesting that for each dollar the stock moved, the option would move $0.62. If I am right on the direction, then, I will profit more quickly because of the higher delta with the LEAPS call than I would with the shorter-term expiration call. Of course, if I am wrong on the direction, I will lose money faster and will need to be aware of precisely when to pull the plug before I ever enter the play.

Since I touched upon the concept of delta, I should also mention that the deeper in the money the option goes, the higher the delta becomes until it approaches 1. In other words, the option can reach the point where it moves nearly dollar for dollar with the price of the stock. When we start a position with a higher delta and it moves in our direction, the delta will approach that 1:1 area more quickly than if we had started with a lower delta. For that reason, when I am buying LEAPS calls, I often choose the strike price that has a delta near 0.70. Again, that is part of my personal business plan. Those calls often are fairly expensive, so you might well decide that you do not need a delta that high on your own entries.

"INSURANCE" FOR SHORT SALES

In Chapter 4, we discussed protective puts. Those puts are the ones to buy as an "insurance policy" in the event stock you own drops in price. What about shorting stock? How can we protect ourselves if we decide to short a stock? One of the answers is to buy protective calls. First, though, let us take a look at how to make money selling stock short.

Selling Stock Short

Many a million has been made by traders selling stock short. What exactly does it mean, and how do we do it? We have all heard the old adage "Buy low and sell high." Undoubtedly, that is the way to make money and that is what most investors try to do. They buy a stock with the belief that it is going to go up in price and they will profit when they sell it. How about reversing the order? If we think a stock is going to go down in price, sell it first; when it drops in price, buy it. We will then have sold high and bought low.

Wait a minute, you say, how can I sell something I do not own? Easy, you borrow the stock from your broker and sell it. First, you need to make sure the broker has the stock in inventory and, depending on the broker, that may require a phone call or it may be as simple as checking on their web site to see if the stock is available to short. If it is, you can place an order to sell the stock short. What that means is that you will borrow the stock and sell it. There is a rule for equities (stocks) that they must be sold on an uptick, but that rarely presents a problem. Since we have borrowed the stock, we will have to return it, so at some point, we will have to buy the stock to "cover" our short position.

Here is what happens. We open the position by borrowing the stock and selling it. Three days later, the money from the sale, less a commission, is in our account. Now we know we have to replace the stock somewhere down the road. What is our goal? We want to have sold it at a high price and have that money come into our account. Then, when the stock falls in price, we want to use the money we got when we opened the position to buy the stock to cover our short position. We get to keep what is left over.

Let us assume that our old friend XYZ stock is trading at $70 a share and it looks like it is going to turn down. We decide to sell XYZ short and, after determining that it is available from our brokerage to short, we place an order to sell 1,000 shares short. Suppose the order is filled at $70. We have sold 1,000 shares of stock we borrowed for $70 a share and three days later, $70,000 comes into our account. If we are right in the stock direction, XYZ begins to fall in price. Say it drops to $50 a share and then looks like it is going to turn back up. Now, using that $70,000 we got when we opened the position, we can "buy to cover" or buy the stock to replace what we borrowed. Since the stock is at only $50 a share, we spend $50,000 plus a commission and close the position. We just made a $20,000 profit on a stock that dropped like a stone.

That seems pretty slick, doesn't it? What is the risk, though? Take the same example, but assume we were wrong about the direction. We sell the stock for $70 a share, but instead of seeing the price fall, we see it climb. Perhaps it even gaps up on some great news and is now trading at $80 or $90 or $100 a share. We borrowed this stock. We are going to have to replace it. If we got $70,000 to open the position, and the stock is now at

$100 a share, it is going to cost us $100,000 to replace it and that means a $30,000 loss. That would not be so much fun, would it? What can we do to try to protect ourselves?

Protective Calls

The call buyer has the right, but not the obligation, to buy the stock at the strike price any time before expiration. Looking at the example of the short sale of XYZ in the preceding section, we see that we have a huge risk if the stock goes up in price instead of down. Theoretically, the price could go up anywhere; there is no limit. Suppose XYZ suddenly announced it had accidentally discovered the cure for cancer. Could the stock go to $500 or more a share? Sure it could, and if we had sold it short, we would have to replace it. Well, if we are going to sell a stock short, we could also buy a call at the same time, couldn't we? If we sold XYZ short at $70 and it had options, we could also buy a $70 or $75 call. By buying such a protective call, we have limited our risk substantially for the life of the call.

In the XYZ example, we are selling 1,000 shares of the stock short at $70 a share and bringing in $70,000. At the same time, let us assume we could buy the $70 calls with an expiration four months away for $2. Instead of having unlimited risk, our risk would now be limited to the premium we paid for the calls. No matter how high or how fast the stock price might climb, if we own the $70 calls, we can buy the stock for $70 any time until expiration. If the stock went to $100 or $500 or whatever, we could exercise our $70 calls and buy to cover our position for the same $70,000 we received when we shorted our stock. We would just be out the premium and some commissions.

Again, as we discussed with protective puts when we buy stock, we do not have to buy an at-the-money call. We could choose a "deductible" and chose to limit our risk by buying some other strike price. If we bought out-of-the-money calls, maybe the $75 call, the premium would be less, but we would be taking on $5 risk ourselves. In any event, our risk would no longer be unlimited. Of course, in order to make a profit, after we had sold the stock short and bought a protective call, the stock price would have to drop more than the price we paid for the premium during the life of the call option.

WRITING COVERED CALLS

An excellent way to make money on a portfolio is to write covered calls. In stock market jargon, *write* or *writing* means to sell. *Covered* means you own the underlying, and you already know what a call is. Generally, the strategy means that you own something (like a stock) and you sell calls on that stock to bring in income. When we sell a call, we receive a premium and obligate ourselves to deliver the stock if "called" at the strike price any time before expiration.

As I write this section, Telik, Inc. (TELK) closed at $16.94. There are two weeks to December expiration, and the December $17.50 call is quoted at $1.50 × $1.65. What does that mean to us? If we liked the stock, we could enter a "buy/write," which means that we could simultaneously buy the stock and sell a call. Using the information above, we could buy the stock for $16.94 and sell the December $17.50 call at the same time. We know from looking at the option price spread that we could sell the calls for at least $1.50 a share. If we decided to open a buy/write, we would pay $16.94 a share for the stock, but since we are selling the call at the same time, it would cost us $16.94 minus $1.50 premium we will receive, or only $15.44 a share. Since we sold the calls, we would be obligated to deliver the stock if it were "called" (or assigned) for the $17.50 strike price any time before expiration. Under what circumstances would it be "called"? No one would want to buy the stock for $17.50 a share if they could get it for less on the open market, so we would expect to be called out of our position only if the stock went above $17.50 a share. Since our net cost (disregarding commission) was $15.44, it would not be too bad to be forced to sell our stock for $17.50, would it? There are only two weeks remaining until the December calls expire, so we could make $2.06 a share or realize a 13.3 percent gain if someone made us sell them our stock for $17.50. What if the stock had gone to $20? We would still have to sell at $17.50 and still would enjoy that 13.3 percent gain, but we would miss out on the extra $2.50. If that bothers you, covered calls may not be for you, but if greater than 13 percent in two weeks seems like something you could live with, this strategy might be one to add to your arsenal.

Suppose the two weeks pass and the stock does not get to $17.50. What happens then? The December $17.50 call would expire worthless and you just keep the $1.50 a share the market paid for the calls you sold—$1.50 on a $16.94 stock price is an 8.8 percent return for two weeks. Now what? Well, you would still own the stock and you just could sell the calls again with a January expiration (or some other expiration). In fact, unless your stock was called, you could keep selling calls every month.

In our TELK example, suppose you had owned the stock for some time and were a buy-and-hold investor. Suppose you bought the stock a year or so earlier when it was trading near $15 and just held on to it before discovering the writing covered call strategy, and that you just are not too keen on watching your stock regularly. Could you consider selling a covered call with an expiration several months away and, perhaps, with a different strike price? Absolutely. Table 5.1 illustrates some of the choices you might make in December.

TABLE 5.1 TELK Calls Table

	Bid	x	Ask
Jan			
15	5.40	×	5.70
17.50	4.40	×	4.70
20	3.50	×	3.70
22.50	2.80	×	2.95
Apr			
15	6	×	6.30
17.50	4.90	×	5.20
20	4	×	4.30
22.50	3.20	×	3.50
Jul			
15	6.20	×	6.60
17.50	5.10	×	5.50
20	4.20	×	4.60

We can see a variety of opportunities. We could choose to sell the April $15 call and bring in $6 a share. In this scenario, we bought the stock for $15, and if we are called out for the price we paid, we would make $6 a share or 40 percent less the commissions. We could select a longer or shorter expiration and a higher or lower strike price as well. We could sell the July $20 calls and bring in $4.20 a share. If the stock went above $20 a share by expiration and we were called out, we would make the $5 a share profit over our original $15 a share cost plus the $4.20 a share premium we received for selling the calls. In that case, we would make $9.20 on our original $15 cost or realize a return of 61 percent.

As Table 5.1 illustrates, we would expect to receive more income if we repeatedly sold the short-term calls each month rather than sell the calls with a longer expiration only once. If we look at the January $17.50 calls, we see we could get $4.40, but if we decided to sell the April $17.50 calls, we would bring in only an additional $0.50 for the extra three months. While it requires more attention, we would bring in more by selling the $17.50 in January, then, assuming we are not called out, selling the February expiration, then the March, and finally the April. I did not show quotes for February or March since those expirations were not yet available. Options expirations are on cycles that differ depending on the stock, but if a stock has options, there is always an expiration for the current month and for the next month as well as whatever other months are in the option cycle. You can always see what expirations are currently available by looking at the option chain. In my TELK example, once the current expiration is January, there will also be a February chain, and once the February chain becomes the current or "front" month, there will then also be a March chain.

In the preceding examples, I used at-the-money and out-of-the-money strikes to demonstrate how calls can be written to bring in income against stock positions. I should mention that an investor can also sell in-the-money calls. If we look at Rambus (RMBS), which was trading around $21.50 in mid-December, we would see that the January $20 calls were trading at $3 × $3.20. If we bought the stock at $21.50 in December and sold those January $20 calls, we would be assuring ourselves of a loss on the stock as long as it stayed above $20 at expiration. However, we would lose only $1.50 a share on the stock, but the market is willing to pay us $3 a share for the call. Overall, then, if we were called out of our position at $20 a share, we would lose $1.50 a share on the stock, but make $3 a share on the calls, for a net gain of $1.50 a share (before commissions). By utilizing that strategy, the stock could drop almost $1.50 and we would still be assured of a profit.

The bottom line in this case is that it would be fine to be called out of our stock, even though we would take a loss on the stock itself, because we would make money overall. In fact, in this real-life example, the net return before commission would be almost 7 percent for six weeks. I do not know about you, but making more than 1 percent per week is okay with me.

Whenever I consider the risk in trading covered calls, it makes me think of my dad. He was born in 1903 and was a true buy-and-hold investor. In fact, he was quite literal about the "hold" part. He had to possess the actual share certificates—it was not enough that his ownership be evidenced by a statement from a brokerage; he kept the certificates in his safe deposit box. He liked to hold them in his hand. Dad was nearing the end of his time when I began to achieve some success trading. He had a fairly large account by then, and I would say to him: "Dad, you should think about writing covered calls against your portfolio." He rarely responded, but one day he said: "Bill, I'm just too old to take those kinds of risks." I stopped in my tracks and asked: "If you buy a stock for $50, what is your risk?" "$50," he answered. "Right," I responded, "but what if you bought a stock for $50 and someone paid you $2 for the right to buy it from you for $55; now what is your risk?" His eyes lit up and he said: "$48. Teach me what to do." He had only about a month left to live then. He was 98 years old, but still very sharp mentally. I was blessed to spend that last month with him, and I was able to do it because I was trading for a living. I was able to trade wherever I could set up my computer. So, for that last month, among the many things about which we spoke, we talked about writing covered calls. He was too sick to ever be able to actually write any calls, but it enabled us to share time I will never forget.

The risk we take when writing covered calls is the price of the stock less the premium we are paid to sell the call. Brokers consider writing covered calls to be a relatively safe strategy as distinguished from selling naked puts. The funny thing is that the risk graph for both strategies is the same. If we sell a naked put and the stock is put to us, the risk is the price of the stock less the premium we have been paid. Brokers will tell you that selling naked puts is a risky strategy. In either case, whether writing covered calls or selling naked puts, the risk is the price of the stock less the premium received. In fact, with the selling naked put strategy, you may not even be put the stock.

WRITING COVERED CALLS AGAINST OPTION POSITIONS

So far, we have discussed writing covered calls when we own the actual stock, but we can still be covered even if we do not own the stock. If we own (or are "long") an option position, we may still be covered. Technically, when we own one option and sell another, we are creating a spread. The effect, however, can be similar to but often better than writing covered calls against a stock. Options provide leverage, as we have seen, so we can buy a call option and control a stock for considerably less than it would cost to buy the stock itself.

As I sit at my computer working on this section, Goldman Sachs (GS) closed the day at $200.20 a share. It would cost a little over $200,000 to buy 1,000 shares of GS stock at that price. Believe it or not, that is more than some people want to commit to a single position. If we did buy 1,000 shares at $200 a share and invested $200,000, our theoretical risk would be $200,000. Now we would be able to sell covered calls against our position. The $220 calls that expire in just over a month are quoted at $2.35 × $2.55, so we could probably get $2.40 a share to sell those covered calls. Ignoring commissions, we would bring in $2,400 on our $200,000 investment, or a return of approximately 1.2 percent for the month. A monthly return of 1.2 percent is certainly better than we are likely to get on a savings account or a CD, but we are at considerable risk if the stock price drops.

On the other hand, the $200 LEAPS calls on GS with an expiration slightly more than two years out are quoted at $35.30 × $36.70. Assuming we could get a little "in between" the spread and buy 10 contracts of these LEAPS calls for $36.30, we would have control of the same 1,000 shares of stock for two years for $36,300 instead of $200,000. By purchasing those calls instead of the stock, we would not receive dividends and we would not get a vote in the corporate elections, but we would control the same 1,000 shares of stock for less than 20 percent of the outlay. Once we owned the calls, we could sell other calls and be covered. We could sell the same $220 calls with expiration a month away and take in the same $2.40 for the month as we could if we owned the stock. One difference, however, is that now instead of a monthly return of only 1.2 percent, we would enjoy a monthly return of 6.6 percent.

In this real-life example, if we chose to invest in the LEAPS calls, we would have a much smaller out-of-pocket investment, a risk limited to what we paid for the calls and a significantly higher percentage return by selling the same shorter-term calls. If we could get around the same 6.6 percent each month selling out-of-the-money calls, we would recoup our complete investment in just 15 months and effectively own our original $200 calls for free with nine months still left until expiration.

If you like that strategy—and, in my opinion, there is a great deal to like—there are a number of things you should consider. As you already know, options do expire, and once the two years in the preceding scenario has passed, we no longer have any rights. In that example, I used the at-the-money calls as the ones being bought. That means the whole premium would be for time value. If the price of the stock did not increase, the time value would erode, relatively slowly at first, and then faster and faster as expiration approached. Of course, if the price of the stock increased, the calls would be gaining intrinsic value and we could expect the value of the option we owned to increase as well, as long as too much time did not elapse. If the stock price reached the point where it exceeded $236.30, our $200 call option would be profitable since the intrinsic value would be higher than the $36.30 we paid in premium. Suppose, for example, that at some point the stock price got to $280 a share. Our $200 call would then be worth at least $80 a share and probably more if there were some time left until expiration, since the premium would include both intrinsic value and time value.

When we have bought a longer-term at-the-money or in-the-money call and are selling shorter-term out-of-the-money calls, we are technically creating what is known as a "diagonal calendar spread." It is a calendar spread because we are taking options positions in two different calendar months. It is considered to be diagonal because we are selling a strike price different from the strike we own.

In the GS example, you saw that I was talking about buying a long-term at-the-money call. I could have just as easily chosen to buy a longer-term in-the-money call, but that would have been more expensive. The same expiration (two years out) $10 in-the-money $190 call was quoted at $40.80 × $42.10, but about $10 or so of that premium was intrinsic value. In either event, there is a significant difference in this diagonal calendar spread strategy from simply writing covered calls against a stock we own. If we own the stock, it is fine if we get called out and have to sell our stock. If we are assigned when we own the stock, we should profit. However, *when we sell a short-term option and own a longer-term option, we do not want to be called out.*

Returning to the GS example where we bought the two-year-out expiration $200 calls for $36.30 and sold the short-term $220 call for $2.40, what would happen if the stock jumped to a price greater than $220 before expiration of the short-term call and we did nothing? We would have paid $36,300 for 10 contracts of the $200 calls and received $2,400 for the $220 calls we sold. We would now be out of pocket $33,900. Now assume the stock went to $230 before our $220 calls expired and we did nothing. What would happen? We could be called out (assigned) at $220. Since we own the $200 calls, we could exercise them at $200, then sell the stock for $220, so we would have a $20-a-share profit or a gain of $20,000 on the stock, but we were in the positions for $33,900, so we would lose $13,900! How could that happen? Because we disposed of our long-term calls by exercising them many months before expiration, we would lose all the remaining time value. Just remember, if we are selling short-term calls against longer-term calls that we own, we want to avoid being called out, since it could cost us all the remaining time value. That is the worst case, and one that we never need suffer. There are some much better alternatives.

The very best alternative is to avoid getting yourself in that fix in the first place. If you own the longer-term $200 calls and have sold the short-term $220 calls, you just need to watch what is happening to the stock price. My first suggestion when you sell the short leg is to sell the shorter-term option with the strike price that is above a resistance. We would expect that a resistance would hold, and, if it does, you are not in any danger of assignment. In our example, let us suppose that there was a resistance at $215 when we sold the $220 call. As the stock price approaches the resistance at $215, it will either retreat or go through the resistance. If it retreats, there is no problem. If it breaks through the resistance, it is wise to act, and act promptly. When the resistance is broken, you are in danger of the stock price going above $220, and, if it goes above $220, you are in danger of assignment and the potential losses outlined earlier. If that happens, let us remove the danger closing the short leg we sold. We just buy to close (buy back) the $220 call leg we sold earlier. If we close that position, we are no longer in danger of being called out. In the example, we sold the short-term $220 calls for $2.40. Depending on how much time has elapsed, we very well might have to take a loss *on that leg* if we have to buy to close the $220 call position.

Let's assume the stock price moved up shortly after we sold the $220 calls and broke above resistance. The stock has reached $216 a share. If the delta on our out-of-the-money $220 calls was 0.40 and the stock went from $200 to $216, the option price may have increased by $6.40 ($16 move in stock times 0.40 delta equals $6.40) so now we have to pay $8.80 to close that leg. We lose $6.40 on that leg. Meanwhile, though, what has been happening to the price of the $200 calls we owned? Naturally, they were going up in price, too. The good news is that they would have a higher delta, since they are longer term and since they started with a strike price that was at-the-money and moved in-the-money as the stock went up in price to $216. Let us assume that the delta of our $200 calls reached 0.65, while the delta of the $220 calls was 0.40. While we were losing $6.40 on the short leg, our long leg was increasing by $10.40 ($16 stock price move times 0.65 delta equals $10.40). We are farther ahead on the leg we still own than we lost on the short leg we closed, and now we are in no danger of being called out. We can now sell another short-term call at an even higher strike price. We just need to take the action and avoid a position where we can be called out when we are employing this diagonal calendar spread strategy. As the old saying goes, we have made lemonade out of lemons.

If, for some reason, you did find yourself in a position where you were assigned on the short leg, the better alternative would be to buy the stock and sell the long LEAPS. In order for us to be called out, the stock would have to be over $220 a share, so let us go back to the assumption that the stock reached $230 a share and we are assigned (called out) at $220. We would buy the stock for $230,000 and sell it for $220,000 (though the numbers are large, this is only a $10,000 difference) and lose $10,000 on that part of the transaction, but we would also sell our 10 contracts of the $200 strike LEAPS calls. We paid $33.90 for them, but the stock quickly went up $30 and we are conservatively assuming a delta of 0.65, so our option price would increase by $19.50 ($30 gain in stock price times 0.65 delta equals $19.50). Now our calls are worth $53.40, so we sell the 10 contracts and bring in $53,400. That is a $19,500 gain on our long LEAPS position, which will be offset by the $10,000 loss on the stock sale, so overall in this example we would enjoy a profit of $9,500. Obviously, that is incredibly better than losing $13,900, as we would if we just exercised our $200 LEAPS, bought the stock at $200,000 and then sold them at the $220 strike where we were called. Again, the lemons would be lemonade.

In the preceding paragraphs, I used a very expensive stock as an example to show that we can control a position for a fraction of the stock price and to demonstrate that even if we are assigned, we can still turn things our way if we just know how. You can use the same strategies with less expensive stocks as well, and I will show an example of that shortly. In the meantime, however, we need to see what we can do if the stock price drops instead of increases.

Continuing with the GS example, suppose the stock drops in price while we own the $200 LEAPS calls. We bought our calls when the stock was trading around $200 a share. If the stock price drops, we have some choices. Before we ever entered our call position we would have decided at what stock price we would exit if the stock went down. I advocate buying stock or calls when the stock price has bounced up off a support or a trend support. The bounce up is some evidence that the support is holding. If the stock price turns down and breaks through the support, the first action could be to sell the calls and take a loss. In Figure 5.1, we can see where the stock price approached the trend and bounced up. That area around $200 is where I bought the LEAPS calls in the example. Now, a break down through that same trend line would be a reason to exit the position.

As we can see, if the stock dropped and the trend was broken at a price around $199, we could immediately sell our calls. We paid $33.90 for the calls and the stock has now dropped $1 in price. If the delta of the at-the-money calls we bought were 0.60, we could lose $0.60 a share by selling our calls for approximately $33.30. On a 10-contract position, that would be a $600 loss plus commissions. Had we owned the stock instead of the calls, our loss would be $1 a share or $1,000. This action would be my first choice. If the trend is broken, I prefer to exit the position, take a little loss and move on to the next trade. Some traders prefer to hang on even if the trend is broken, and while that is not my first choice, shorter-term options can still be sold against the position.

If the stock dropped to $180 a share, for example, the $200 strike would be two strikes out-of-the-money. We saw earlier that the two-strike out-of-the-money call about a month from expiration was trading for about $2.40, so we could probably sell the near-month $200 strike for somewhere between $2 and $2.40. We would then be creating a calendar spread by owning the long term and selling the shorter term. This spread would be a calendar spread rather than a diagonal calendar spread because we would own the $200 strike and sell the $200 strike, but for different expiration

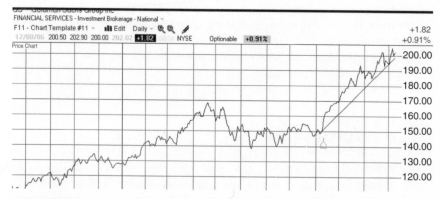

FIGURE 5.1 Using Trend Entry and Exit for LEAPS. (Telechart 2005® chart courtesy of Worden Brothers, Inc.)

months. As we saw in the beginning of these examples, if we could get about $2.40 a month selling two-strike out-of-the-money calls, we would recoup our original investment in about 15 months and we would still own the calls with which we started, but at no net cost.

As we have seen, many combinations are possible using this spreading strategy. As of the time of this writing, NVIDIA (NVDA) was trading around $35.80. The out-of-the-money $40 calls with a year to expiration were quoted at $5.90 × $6.10. At the same time, the same strike $40 calls with an expiration about a month away were trading for $0.75 × $0.80. I should mention that there are also $37.50 strikes on NVDA, so the $40 calls are two strikes out-of-the-money. If an investor could get $0.75 a month each month selling a strike price well out of the money on a $6.10 investment (which is exactly what is available as I write this section), she would be realizing about 12.3 percent per month before commission and would regain her complete original cost in eight or nine months.

Though there is some advantage to selling the near-month calls each month, an investor could also choose to sell an option with a longer term in order to avoid the necessity of trading each month. In the NVDA case, the $40 calls with an expiration roughly six months away were quoted at $3.60 × $3.70, so a trader could buy the one-year-out $40 strike for $6.10 and, at the same time, sell the six-month expiration for $3.60 for a net entry cost of only $2.50 plus commissions. If the stock price were below $40 at expiration of the six-month short position, that short leg would expire worthless and the trader could sell more options either on a monthly basis or out to expiration of the longer-term leg.

This overall strategy is one I use regularly. It provides the ability to generate monthly income and has a potential for high rewards. As discussed earlier, countermeasures sometimes may be necessary, depending on stock movement, so it does require some tending, but I have found that the effort is well worth it. As with all strategies, you should understand it completely before trading real money. If you like what you see, practice the strategy by virtual trading or paper trading without real money. See how you are doing and learn from your mistakes before putting real cash at risk. When you have successfully practiced and learned this one, I think you will like it as much as I do.

SELLING NAKED CALLS

In Chapter 4, we discussed the strategy of selling naked puts in some detail. It is a strategy I often use in a bullish market on bullish stocks. Since we undertake the obligation to buy the stock at the strike price when we sell naked puts, the risk is limited and is equivalent to the price of the stock less the premium received when selling the put.

Selling naked calls is a strategy that is available when a trader believes a stock is going to go down in price. It is a strategy that I just do not use. Here, I agree completely with the brokers who consider the strategy to be risky. Selling naked calls is reserved for those Level 5 traders who are willing to take on potentially huge risks for relatively small and limited rewards. When a trader sells a naked call, he owns no stock but takes on the obligation to sell the stock at the strike price at any time before expiration. He receives a premium for selling the call, and that is the maximum reward he can get. The risk, however, is theoretically unlimited.

To illustrate the danger inherent in selling a naked call, we can look at a stock like Google (GOOG). GOOG has been a pretty pricey stock with some hefty option premiums. In the middle of October 2005, it had been bumping along against a resistance in the $310 to $320 range. On October 20, it closed at $303.20. Suppose we decided to sell five contracts of the $310 strike calls that day. If we were naked, we had no stock, so we collected a premium and obligated ourselves to deliver the stock at $310 anytime before expiration if called. The next morning, the stock gapped up to open at $345.80. By November 28, it closed at just above $423. Whatever premium we got was soon erased by the sharp upward move of the stock price. The stock moved up about $120 a share in a month. We agreed to sell the stock at $310 a share for five contracts (500 shares), but we had no stock. In order to sell the stock, we would have to buy it at the current price if called. The current price is $423, so we will lose $113 a share or $56,500 (less the premium we took in) when we sell the stock at the $310 price at which we obligated ourselves to deliver.

GOOG is only one of a myriad of examples of the danger inherent in selling naked calls. In slightly more than a month beginning in September 2006, GS moved almost 35 points in a very steep climb. In fact, by December it had climbed around $50.

The problem with the naked call is that there is great risk without any protection if the stock moves up. I just avoid the strategy. In the next section, we see how to use calls to profit on a downward price movement and still limit the risk significantly.

CASH IN ON A DOWNWARD MOVE

In Chapter 4, we saw how we can profit from a downward move using directional puts. Now, we explore a spread using calls that can be very productive, sometimes very quickly. As you have already learned, a spread is a strategy with two or more legs. When we examined selling shorter-term calls against a long-term or LEAPS position we owned (or were "long"), we saw an example of a calendar spread that is known as a horizontal spread. It is called a horizontal spread because positions are entered "horizontally" in two different months. In Chapter 4, we investigated the bullish put spread where we sold a put at one strike and bought another put at a lower strike, but both in the same expiration month. That type of spread is known as a vertical spread. In the vertical spread, we are buying and selling different strikes but in the same month.

Now we look at another vertical spread—one that uses calls and enables us to profit from a stock whose price stays the same or goes down (and in some cases, even if the price goes up a bit). I am referring to the bearish call spread. Bearish suggests that the market, sector, and/or stock price is going down in price. When we use a bearish call spread, we want to take advantage of that movement. Though we sell one leg in the bearish call spread to bring in income, we do not run the same risk as we do with selling a naked call, since we also buy another, protective, leg. We are selling the leg with the lower strike to bring in income, and we are buying the leg with the higher strike for protection. Since the leg we are selling (the one with the lower strike) will be more expensive than the leg we are buying (the one with the higher strike), we will open the position for a credit. In other words, cash will come into our account when we open these two positions together.

Again, we can look at an example to see how the strategy works. With about five weeks to January expiration, NVIDIA (NVDA) was trading below $36, and had bounced down from a resistance near $37.50. I was able to sell the short-term $37.50 call for $1.50. By selling 10 contracts of the $37.50s, I received $1,500 in premium ($1.50 a share times 10 contracts times 100 shares per contract) and undertook the obligation to deliver the stock if called (assigned) at $37.50 a share.

If that were all I had done, I would have sold a naked call and exposed myself to the tremendous risks outlined above. However, instead of just selling the $37.50 call, I also bought the $40 call with the same expiration for $0.75. The leg I bought now offered protection in the event the stock price jumped. I brought in $1,500 and paid out $750 for a net before commissions of $750. Before receiving any money, my risk would be only $2,500. If I were called out of the stock and had to sell it for $37.50 ($37,500 for 1,000 shares), I could exercise my own $40 calls, buy the stock for $40,000 and have only a $2,500 loss. Clearly, the risk was significantly less than the theoretically unlimited risk had I chosen to simply sell a naked call. However, my real risk was not $2,500, since the market, in effect, paid me $750 to take the risk. Therefore, my real risk was $2,500 less the $750 I received in net premium or $1,750. Now, my return on risk for five weeks was a whopping 42.8 percent ($750 cash-in divided by $1,750 risk)! As long as the stock was below $37.50 at expiration and I made no adjustment before expiration, I would enjoy a five-week return of over 42 percent. The $37.50 calls I sold certainly would not be exercised unless the stock price went higher than $37.50. I would keep all of the $750 (less the commissions) if the stock price stayed the same as it were when I entered the position (under $36), if the stock price went down, and even if it went up, as long as it was not above $37.50 at expiration.

Admittedly, this trade provided a pretty good rate of return on risk, but such returns are not rare. Spreads entered with four or five weeks to expiration with potential returns on risk in the 30 to 40 percent range are not too unusual.

As in the case of the bullish put spread, when I enter a bearish call spread, my job is to keep all or as much of the initial credit as possible. In my NVDA trade, as long as the stock stays below $37.50 until the options expire, I have nothing to do. However, what happens if the stock does go above $37.50? Now I could be called and have to sell stock at $37.50. I have a number of options (no pun intended). If there is a lot of time left, I can simply do nothing and see what happens. If there is little time left until expiration and I have no specific reason to believe the stock will drop again quickly, I could unwind the whole position. I would do that by buying to close the $37.50 calls I am short and selling to close the $40 calls I am long. If I choose that course of action, I will probably reduce my loss below the maximum possible and be out of the whole position. If there were a lot of time left and it looked like the stock was going to continue to climb, I could buy to close my short $37.50 leg (the one I sold to open in the beginning) and hold on to the $40 leg. If the stock price continues up, that long leg should gain in value and I could reduce my loss and, if the stock price moved up enough, even turn the whole trade into a gain. It is really cool when a play goes against you and you still turn it into something profitable. You do need to be aware that selecting the last alternative of closing the short leg and retaining the long leg can result in a greater loss than just closing the whole trade out when it moved against us. Once the short leg has been closed, the risk can increase since the value of the long leg can go to zero if the stock price turns back down. For me, the bottom line is that I prefer to close the whole position (both legs) if the stock price moves up above resistance unless there is a lot of time left (like three weeks or more).

In Chapter 4, we examined buying a put option to attempt to profit from a downward move in the stock price. You probably recall that, in order to profit with the put, the stock had to move down (and relatively quickly) in order for the trade to be successful. Compare that strategy to the bearish call spread where we would make money if the stock went down, stayed the same, or as in our NVDA example, even if it went up to $37.45.

SUMMARY

This chapter covered a number of ways to make money with calls. We have seen how we can use the long call, especially LEAPS, as a cheaper substitute for buying a stock. We have explored ways to generate income by writing covered calls against stock we own. We see how we can open calendar spreads where we own a longer-term call and sell shorter-term calls against that position to generate income. In addition, we have seen the significant risks of writing naked calls, but have learned how to reduce that risk to manageable proportion and, at the same time, generate some really great returns on bearish call spreads when we want to capitalize on a downward movement.

In Chapter 6, we look at some ways to combine the strategies from Chapters 4 and 5 to create some very low-risk—even zero-risk—plays that can provide handsome profits without much (or any) worry on the investor's part.

Combining Strategies for No-Risk and Low-Risk Trades

In Chapter 4, we examined the protective put as a way to "insure" a long stock position, and in Chapter 5, we saw how we could generate some income by writing covered calls. One of the downsides of protective puts was the cost of the premium to purchase the protection. Now we look at selling the covered call in conjunction with buying the protective put so that the premium received from selling the call pays for most or all of the premium for the put. We will even look at circumstances where we not only take in enough from the call premium to pay for the protective put, but also have a credit left over. Many times, these "collars" can even be constructed so that there is literally no risk in the play.

I will also cover the "iron condor," a limited-risk strategy used to produce income on a stock that is moving sideways within a channel.

Finally, we will investigate the concept of volatility and introduce the straddle and strangle, which are limited-risk, nondirectional trades with theoretically unlimited rewards.

COLLARS

The collar is a three-pronged position where we buy the stock, buy a protective put, and sell a call all at the same time. Generally, we seek to find situations where we can buy a stock that looks like it is going up and, at the same time, buy at-the-money or slightly out-of-the-money protective puts and sell out-of-the-money calls whose premium equals or exceeds the premium we pay for the puts. Quite often, the puts we are buying and the calls we are selling have expirations a year or even two years out, though, occasionally, shorter-term expirations do work. Often, we can locate zero-risk collars, and sometimes we are able to construct a collar that is even better than *zero risk!* We can even find positions where a profit is guaranteed at the time of entry.

As I write this chapter, Amazon (AMZN) closed at $40 a share. The $40 LEAPS put (exactly one year to expiration) is trading at $5 × $5.20, and the $42.50 LEAPS calls (same expiration) are quoted at $5.80 × $6. We could buy the stock at $40 a share, buy the $40 puts for $5.20, and sell the $42.50 calls for $5.80. Since we could sell the stock at $40 by exercising our $40 puts, we would have no risk no matter how low the stock fell. Until expiration, we could always sell the stock for the same amount we paid. In effect, the protection cost us nothing because we would take in more for selling the calls than we would pay for the puts. We bought the puts for $5.20 and sold the calls (with a $2.50 higher strike) for at least $5.80. The absolute worst thing that can happen to us is that we will make $0.60 a share. So, no matter whether the stock goes up, down, or sideways over the next year, we can't do worse than make $0.60. We have put ourselves in a position where the absolute worst-case scenario yields 1.5 percent. The best case would occur if AMZN went above $42.50 at expiration and we were called out. In that case, we would make $2.50 a share on the stock (bought it at $40, called out at $42.50) plus the $0.60 or $3.10 a share. That would result in a 7.75 percent return on a play that could not lose in the worst case.

Collars have numerous advantages, particularly for the investor whose first priority is preservation of capital. As we have just seen, collars can be constructed that actually assure a profit from the outset no matter what happens to the stock price over the life of the options. They can afford zero-risk opportunities. Once the collar is found and established, the investor has little or nothing to do until expiration. At times, collars can be found that offer potential gains of as high as 30 percent to rarely 50 percent. The collar strategy is one in which I would consider buying on margin, though margin buying is something I usually avoid.

Buying on Margin

So far, I have made no mention of margin use by the trader or investor. Buying on margin entails borrowing up to half the stock purchase price from your broker. Of course, the broker charges interest on the amount borrowed. When an investor buys on margin, he gains leverage if the stock moves up in price, but, no matter what the stock does, he will have to pay back the money borrowed from the broker. Margin buying can be wonderful when a stock increases in value, but devastating if the price falls.

If I bought 1,000 shares of XYZ at $20 a share, it would cost me $20,000. If I bought the same 1,000 shares on margin, I would have to put up only $10,000 and would borrow the other $10,000 from my broker. As long as the stock goes up, I am a happy camper. If the stock goes to $25 and I sell, I repay the $10,000 and have $15,000 in my account. I made $5,000 on my $10,000 or a 50 percent return on my money. Had I bought the stock for cash, I would have invested $20,000 and still made $5,000, but that would only be a 25 percent return. So far, margin sounds pretty good, but what if the stock fell in price instead? Suppose I bought the same 1,000 shares at $20 on margin and the stock fell to $15. Now the position is only worth $15,000 and I still have to repay the $10,000 I borrowed. I have lost $5,000 of my $10,000, or 50 percent of my investment. Again, had I paid cash, I would still be down $5,000, but that would only be a 25 percent loss. An even greater problem occurs if the drop in stock is more significant.

Suppose, in our example, that the stock dropped to $10 a share. Now the position is worth only $10,000, but I still owe that to the broker. I have now lost 100 percent of my original investment, and the value of the stock would just be enough to repay the loan. In order to protect brokerage firms in situations like this, the National Association of Security Dealers (NASD) and the New York Stock Exchange (NYSE) require investors to maintain a margin account balance of at least 25 percent of the market price of any stock they buy. In fact, some individual brokerage houses require an even higher margin level. If the market value of the stock falls below the minimum, the investor gets a margin call to add the amount of money necessary to meet the minimum. If the call is not met, the stock is sold to pay back the broker.

Looking at the last part of the example, where the stock dropped to $10 from the $20 entry, I would no longer have any equity in the position since I put up only $10,000 in the first place. If my broker had a 25 percent margin requirement, I would have to add $2,500 (25 percent times $10,000 current market price) to meet the margin call, or the stock would be sold and I would lose all of my original investment.

Additional Considerations When Placing Collars

As we have seen, when we put on a collar, one of the elements is a protective put, so we are not running the risk of a margin call if we buy the stock on margin. We do need to understand and be aware that we are paying interest on the loan the broker has made, so if we do buy the stock on margin, we want to be sure that we account for the margin interest costs in calculating our potential profits. One of the problems with collars is that

TABLE 6.1	LEAPS Premiums on Altera	
CALLS	**Strike**	**PUTS**
$5.80 × $6.00	17.50	$1.75 × $1.95
$4.50 × $4.70	20	$2.80 × $2.95
$3.40 × $3.60	22.50	$4.00 × $4.30
$2.50 × $2.75	25	$5.70 × $5.90

they can be expensive to enter since the cost of buying a stock may be high and a great deal of capital may be required. Utilizing margin is a way to reduce the amount of capital devoted to a given trade or a way to increase the number of shares purchased for a given collar.

When creating a collar, the investor has a variety of choices to make. First, is he willing to take any risk at all, and, if so, how much? Since calls will be sold, the possible gain will be capped at the strike price of the calls. Where will that cap be placed? Does the investor demand that the entire premium for the puts be recouped by the sale price of the calls, or is it sufficient to simply reduce that cost? We can look at an example to see the process of determining what collar to create. Table 6.1 shows the put and call premiums for LEAPS on Altera (ALTR), which was then trading at $20.

If we decided we wanted to enter a zero-risk trade, we could buy the $20 LEAPS puts for $2.95 and sell the $22.50 calls for $3.40. The calls we sold would pay for the puts and we would have $0.45 left over. No matter what, the worst case would be that we could assign the stock for the same $20 we paid for it and we would still be up the $0.45 credit of the call sale over the put buy. We would realize a very modest 2.25 percent gain even if the stock went completely south. On the other hand, if the stock went above $22.50 by expiration, we would make a $2.50-a-share profit on the stock plus the $0.45 we got at entry, for an overall return of 14.75 percent. That trade would have no risk, assure a small gain at worst, and offer a decent, if conservative, return at best. If we are willing to take a little risk, however, we can place ourselves in a position to enjoy a greater potential return.

We could still buy the $20 LEAPS puts for $2.95, but instead of selling the $22.50 calls, we could sell the $25 calls for $2.50. In that event, the call premium we get would not quite cover the premium for the puts; we would wind up paying $0.45 net to own the $20 puts. Now the worst case would be that the stock falls and we put it to someone at the same $20 we paid, but the "insurance" wound up costing us $0.45. On the brighter side, however, if the stock runs up to $25 or more by expiration, we make $5 a share minus the $0.45 protection cost, or $4.55 a share. That would result in a 22.75 percent return on a very low-risk play. Obviously, the choice is always yours. You are balancing risk against potential reward.

If we thought the stock were likely to increase in value, we might consider taking on even a bit more risk to increase the potential reward. Instead of buying the at-the-money put, we could buy the out-of-the-money $17.50 put for $1.95. If we did that and sold the $25 calls for $2.50, we would have paid for the protection and have $0.55 left over. Since we bought the stock at $20, our risk would now be $1.95 (our cost of $20 minus $17.50 at which we could assign the stock plus $0.55 premium left over from selling the call). If called at $25, though, we would now make $5 a share on the stock plus the $0.55, or a return of 27.75 percent.

As a last example using ALTR, suppose we bought the stock at $20, bought the $2.50 in-the money $22.50 puts for $4.30, and sold the $25 calls for $2.50. Where would we be? Well, again, we would be in a "can't lose" position if we hold until expiration. The puts would cost us $1.80 more than the calls, but we would be able to put the stock to someone for $2.50 more than we paid for the stock, so we would make $0.70 if we did that. If the stock were called at $25, we would make $5 a share on the stock less the $1.80 difference between the put and call price, or $3.20 a share.

Collars can be used with any price stock as long as the stock has options with at least some open interest. In most cases, the open interest necessary for me to enter a collar is less than if I am trading an option directionally. If I am trading options directionally, I want a fair amount of open interest so I know there is enough liquidity to get out if I want to or need to exit. Since I usually expect to be in a collar for a fairly long amount of time, the liquidity is not as critical. Often, the open interest in LEAPS may be less than in the shorter-term options and increases as time goes on. In a collar, I normally have bought the puts, so I can assign my stock if necessary, and the calls have been used to bring in enough income to pay for the puts. In those circumstances, open interest over 50 or 75 contracts satisfies me as long as the bid-ask spread is not too great.

I frequently use collars to park relatively large amounts of money where I want my capital protected and have a good potential upside. I have found in recent times that expensive stocks have worked well for me. Before providing some examples, I should mention that I have spoken to several amateur traders who shy away from the expensive stocks even though they may have the money to buy them. Many people prefer to buy stock that trades in the $20- to $60-a-share range rather than buy stocks that trade for $100 or more. "I can buy 500 shares of a $20 stock for $10,000, but only 100 shares of a $100 stock," they say. I say, "So what?" If the stock moves up 10 percent, you make $1,000 in either case. I have found some nice collars with the more expensive stocks, and I believe they are at least worth looking at when you are trying to find good collars to invest some safe money.

In May, for example, I bought 200 shares of GOOG for $231 a share (that tells you how long ago) and, at the same time, bought the LEAPS $230 puts for $36.30 and sold the $250 calls for $40.40. At the time I entered the collar, expiration was a year and a half away. The calls I sold paid for my puts and I had $4.10 a share left over. I wanted to park some money safely and give myself a chance to enjoy some appreciation if the stock moved up. I accomplished what I wanted. I invested $46,200 in a situation where the worst thing that could happen was that I would make $4.10 a share even if GOOG tanked. If I stayed until expiration and the stock were above $250, I would make another $19 a share, or a total of $23.10 a share (before commissions), for a return of 10 percent. In my view, that was not a bad trade considering that the worst possible situation would still result in a profit of $4.10 a share. I had no risk and a potential upside of 10 percent. A conservative investor would have to like that trade.

Just because you enter a collar does not mean you have to stay in it until expiration. In the GOOG trade I just related, the stock soared. I bought it in May for $231 and by July it was trading near $380 a share. I saw an opportunity to exit the trade and make more than I expected and much more than I would have if I had just left the collar in place. With the stock trading at $380, I unwound everything. Here is what I did: I had bought the $230 puts for $36.30. Since the stock had gone way up in price, the puts were worth less, but since there was a lot of time left, they still had some decent value and I was able to sell them for $21.70. I lost $14.60 on the puts. Since the stock price had rocketed, the calls went up in price and I paid $61.20 to buy to close the calls. I lost $20.80 on the calls. However, the stock had gone up $149 a share in price so I sold the stock at $380 and made $149 on the stock. This was the final tally:

Stock sale	$149.00	Profit
Put sale	−$14.60	Loss
Buy-back calls	−$20.80	Loss
Net Profit/Share	**$113.60**	**Overall profit**

By unwinding the position about two months after I entered, I was able to realize a gain of $113.60 a share, or a return of 58.9 percent in only two months—and I never had any risk at all! This trade made more than $22,700 on a $46,200 investment—over $11,000 a month profit. As Larry the Cable Guy might say: "I don't care who you are, that's a good trade."

One of the difficulties with collars is that the best ones may be hard to find. There is no question but that it is worth looking for them if you want really safe limited- or no-risk investments with good potential. I am looking at one right now on Chicago Mercantile Exchange Holdings, Inc. (CME). The stock is trading at a lofty $533 a share, so 100 shares will cost $53,300. The $530 LEAPS puts with a one-year-out expiration can be bought for about $61, and the same expiration $560 calls can be sold for around $65. Ignoring the relatively small commissions, I can set up this position where my greatest risk is that I will make a $4-a-share profit and I have a potential upside of about $34 a share if the stock is above $560 and I hold until expiration. Of course, as we saw in the GOOG example, there is nothing to prevent me from unwinding profitably if the stock happens to go on a quick run. Meanwhile, my money is as safe as it can be. Of course, this particular trade will not be available by the time this book is published and you are reading it, but there will be other trades that are every bit as good and maybe quite a bit better. You just need to look and keep looking. If you are willing to persist, your persistence will be rewarded.

Although I have used examples involving high-priced stocks, collars can be placed on stocks of any price, so do not be put off thinking that the strategy applies only to the pricier equities. Even stocks priced under $10 may offer good collar opportunities. As I write, for example, I see that Level 3 (LVLT) is trading at $5.95. The one-year-out $5 puts are selling for $0.75, and the $7.50 calls are going for $0.90. With a two-year expiration, the $5 puts are at $1.10 and the $7.50 calls are $1.45. A search of stocks in the price range you want will yield good collar candidates if you are willing to make the effort to find them.

While collars have many advantages, I should note that in addition to sometimes requiring a high capital outlay and being difficult to find, the gain is normally limited to the strike of the calls that are sold and they often must be held until expiration. I have not figured out why, but I find that it seems easiest to find good collars in mid to late summer and early fall. For practical purposes, that means that the option positions I usually enter are LEAPS that expire about a year and a half from the time I open the trade.

When a collar is placed, normally all three positions are entered simultaneously. I sometimes deviate from that practice to try to get a bigger bang for my buck. There are times when I will buy a stock that is trending up and, at the same time, buy a protective put. Instead of selling the call right away, I will wait until the stock goes up farther and turns down. Since the stock price is then greater than the price I paid, the calls are also more expensive, so I can realize a higher premium for the same strike or I can sell an even higher strike call and still get a premium sufficient to pay for my puts. Another variation I occasionally use is to buy the stock and protective put and then sell out-of-the-money calls each month rather than selling the LEAPS call just once. As we saw in Chapter 5, if we sell the calls each month, we ultimately take in more money than we would if we sold the call only once with a longer expiration. No matter how we do it, the goal with the collar is to place ourselves in a small- or no-risk situation while still providing a substantial upside potential.

IRON CONDOR

While the collar is generally a long-term low-risk or no-risk trade, the iron condor is a very short-term limited-risk trade. In placing an iron condor, we are looking for an optionable stock that is running sideways or consolidating in a relatively flat channel. When an appropriate candidate is found, we will combine two of the strategies explained earlier. We will enter a bullish put spread as described in Chapter 4 and a bearish call spread as explained in Chapter 5. Since both of these spreads are entered for a credit, we will, in essence, bring in about twice the credit as we would if we entered either spread by itself.

As an example, the NYSE Euronext (NYX) had been channeling between about $95 and $110 for more than a month. The stock had just closed around $101 and there was a little less than a month to expiration. I wanted to look at an iron condor where I would be placing a bearish call spread where the call I was selling was just above resistance and placing a bullish put spread where the put I was selling would be just below a support. Since there was support at $95, I would consider a $95/$90 bullish put spread and with resistance at $110, a $110/$115 bearish call spread. The near-month $95 puts were selling for about $3, and the $90 puts would cost me about $1.70, so I could get a $1.30 credit for the bullish put spread. On the other side, the $110 calls would bring in about $2.40, while the $115 calls would cost $1.45, so I could bring in an additional credit of $0.95. Overall, placing the iron condor with a $110/$115 bearish call spread and a $95/$90 bullish put spread would bring in a credit, before commissions of $2.25. If we did 10 contracts of each leg, that would mean the $2,250 less commissions would come into my account the next day. As long as the stock price stayed between $95 and $110 until expiration, I would be able to keep the whole credit since all the options would expire worthless. Here is what the positions would look like:

Long 115 Calls = −$1.45
Short 110 Calls = +$2.40
Short 95 Puts = +$3.00
Long 90 Puts = −$1.70

Net Credit = +$2.25

Of course, even if Murphy's Law went into operation, only one side of the iron condor could be a loser at expiration. Obviously, the stock could not close at expiration both higher than $110 and lower than $95, so either the bullish put spread or the bearish call spread would expire worthless and the complete credit from that side would be kept even in a worst-case scenario.

The maximum risk in the trade occurs when the stock is either above the long call strike or below the long put strike. The risk is calculated by subtracting the credit obtained ($2.25 in our case) from the difference between the strikes of the puts or calls ($5 in our examples, since the puts were $95 × $90 and the calls were $110 × $115) times the number of shares. In our example, we used 10 contracts, so the maximum risk would be $5 minus $2.25 equals $2.75 times 1,000 (10 contracts times 100 shares per contract) equals $2,750. Again, ignoring commissions, we can see that the return on risk (ROR) is $2,250 credit at initiation divided by $2,750 risk or a delightful 81.8 percent for less than a month provided the stock stays between $95 and $110.

If we were willing to take a lesser credit, we could reduce the risk of losing on either side of the iron condor. Google had been trading between about $450 and $510 a share. With three weeks to expiration, we could have chosen to place an iron condor using the $450 support and the $510 resistance. If that were our choice, the trade would look something like this:

$$
\begin{aligned}
\text{Buy } \$520 \text{ call} &= -\$1.15 \\
\text{Sell } \$510 \text{ call} &= +\$1.75 \\
\text{Sell } \$450 \text{ put} &= +\$5.90 \\
\text{Buy } \$440 \text{ put} &= -\$3.70 \\
\hline
\end{aligned}
$$

Net Credit before commissions = +$2.80

Using the formula discussed above to determine risk, we would subtract the credit received ($2.80) from the difference in the strikes of the puts or the calls ($10) to see that we would have a maximum risk of $7.20 a share. Since we would have a credit of $2.80 a share, our three-week return on risk would equal 38.8 percent ($2.80 divided by $7.20) as long as the stock price remained between the $450 support and the $510 resistance at expiration. Suppose we wanted to be a bit more cautious and decided to increase the spread between the short calls and the short puts by $20. Now we would be selling the $520 calls and the $440 puts, so we would have no risk as long as the stock traded between $520 and $440 over the next three weeks or at least closed between $520 and $440 at expiration. The following would be our situation:

$$
\begin{aligned}
\text{Buy } \$530\,\text{call} &= -\$0.70 \\
\text{Sell } \$520\,\text{call} &= +\$1.10 \\
\text{Sell } \$440\,\text{put} &= +\$3.60 \\
\text{Buy } \$430\,\text{put} &= -\$2.15 \\
\hline
\text{Net Credit before commissions} &= +\$1.85
\end{aligned}
$$

Now our credit is reduced from $2.80 a share to $1.85 a share, but we have increased our area of safety. Now, instead of risking loss if the stock is above $510 or below $450, we have no risk unless the stock goes above $520 at expiration or below $440. We have increased the "safety zone" by $20. We calculate risk the same way, by subtracting the credit ($1.85 in this case) from the difference in strikes between the calls or the puts (still $10), so now our risk is $8.85 a share and our return on risk would be 20.9 percent; still pretty good for a three-week play. While the dollar amount of risk has increased, the likelihood that the position will incur loss has decreased since we widened the distance of safety. Now the stock can move farther up or down before we would be exposed to loss.

Some of the things I really like about iron condors are that they bring in a credit when opened and they are usually of short duration. One of the things I dislike is that I am utilizing four positions and that means at least four commissions. I say at least four commissions because the possibility exists that I could also buy to close a short position or positions if there is a reasonable possibility that they could expire in-the-money. For example, if the stock dropped below the strike price of the put I had sold, I would buy that leg to close it and would also sell the lower-strike long put if it had value. Those actions would incur additional commissions. Of course, if the stock were dropping near expiration and I closed the put side of the iron condor, I could probably leave the call side alone and allow those options to expire worthless. The opposite would be true if the stock ran up in price. I then might close the call side and let the puts expire.

Even when the stock price is where I want it to be between the short calls (the ones I sold) and the short puts (also the ones I sold) and nearing expiration, I very well may decide to buy to close those positions. Remember, each of those options I sold were out-of-the-money, so all I sold was time value. As time passes, the time value diminishes, so I would expect that I could close each leg by buying it back for less than I sold it. If I can assure a profit in that fashion and also eliminate the risk, it can be a good way to go.

VOLATILITY

In all option trades, consideration should be given to volatility. I think of volatility as the speed of movement of the underlying security. There are two types of volatility. The first, known as historical or statistical volatility (SV), is what has already happened and can be measured. The other is implied volatility (IV), and without going into a long-winded technical explanation, it is the market's prediction of what the volatility will be in the future.

Volatilities are expressed in percentages and, therefore, essentially go between 0 and 100 percent. Volatilities have a proven tendency to regress to the mean, and that can give us some important information about pricing.

In general, when we are buying an option, we would probably prefer to buy a cheap option, but the question becomes: What does "cheap" mean? An option selling for $1 is not necessarily cheap, and one selling for $15 is not necessarily expensive. "Cheap" options are those that are in the lower percentiles of IV. Please note that I refer to the *percentile*, not the raw percentage of IV. In order to know the percentile, we must have a history of the IV (not to be confused with historical volatility or SV) so we can see where it currently falls in comparison to past readings. Once we see that IV is in the lower percentiles, we know the option price is relatively cheap, so we can consider buying it.

By comparing IV to SV, we can also see whether the option is currently fairly valued, undervalued, or overvalued. Quite simply, if IV is the same as SV, the option is probably close to fair value. If IV is less than SV, it is probably undervalued, so if IV is in the lower percentiles and is below SV, we have a relatively cheap, undervalued option.

For an excellent and in-depth discussion of volatility trading, I would suggest Lawrence G. McMillan, *Options as a Strategic Investment* (4th ed., New York Institute of Finance, 2002).

TRADING VOLATILITY—STRADDLES AND STRANGLES

By applying the principles in the preceding section, we can see how we could buy cheap, undervalued options or sell expensive, overpriced options. One commonly used strategy to trade volatility is the straddle. A straddle is a two-legged position where the trader buys both puts and calls with the same strike price and the same expiration on a given stock. If the stock moves rapidly in one direction or the other and/or if there is an increase in volatility, the trader expects to make money. The trader does not care in which direction the stock price moves as long as it moves (the faster and the farther, the better) and/or if there is an increase in IV. In general, the trader will seek stocks where the IV is in the lower percentiles and is beneath the SV. If IV increases, both the price of the puts and the price of the calls can increase as well.

Risk in buying a straddle is limited to the price paid for the calls plus the price paid for the puts plus commissions. The maximum risk is realized only if both positions are held to expiration and the stock price closes at expiration at exactly the strike price purchased. Potential gains are unlimited (except on the put side where the maximum gain arises if the stock price goes to zero).

Strangles are similar to straddles except that the strike price of the call purchased is different from the strike price of the put. In this situation, risk is again limited to the initial investment, but is over a wider range. If the trader bought the January $40 calls and the January $30 puts on XYZ, the maximum loss would be realized if held to expiration if the stock price fell between $40 and $50. Strangles are generally less expensive to enter since the options that are bought are each usually out-of-the-money, while with the straddle they are usually at-the-money. Though less expensive to buy, the stock price and/or IV must experience a greater move for a strangle to profit than would be necessary for a straddle to profit.

Each of these strategies is nondirectional (at least we don't care which direction as long as we get sufficient movement) and has limited risk and potentially unlimited reward (except on the put side, where the reward is limited only by the stock price's reaching zero). When entering either of these strategies, I like to give the stock price enough time to move so I normally take positions with an expiration from 4 to 10 months out.

SUMMARY

The collar offers the chance to enter a combination of positions that can offer high returns with little or no risk. Sometimes, we can create a collar that assures a worst-case scenario where we will make a little money. In other words, a collar can be a play that guarantees a profit no matter what happens to our stock and still can have a very high upside potential. At the same time, when using collars, we do limit the upside in exchange for safety.

Iron condors, unlike collars, are usually very short-term positions. This strategy enables the trader to find some pretty good short-term returns with known limited risk and a credit at entry. Iron condors provide one way to profit on stocks that are channeling or rolling within a fairly tight range.

Straddles and strangles are medium-length positions that provide limited-risk, nondirectional plays and are often entered as pure volatility plays. They each have theoretically unlimited rewards.

The last three chapters have explored ways to make money when a stock is going up, when it is going down, and even when it is moving sideways. There are not any other choices. We have seen how risk can be limited and even removed entirely. Keep these principles in mind and use them in developing your own business plan. You will like some of those strategies, you will love others, and some will not be for you. Choose the ones that fit your trading personality and the time you can devote. You do not have to know every strategy intimately; you do need to know completely those you are going to trade with real money.

There is nothing wrong with using only one strategy. Just remember that if you are going to use nothing but a bullish strategy, you are not going to trade all the time. You are going to trade only when conditions are bullish. The same is true if you like only a bearish strategy. Use it only when conditions are bearish. Of course, you now know several bullish strategies, several bearish strategies, and some neutral strategies. If you like a strategy in each category (up, down, or sideways), you can trade any time you choose. Just be sure let the market guide you in choosing the right strategy for the direction the markets are moving.

In Chapter 7, we look at some relatively nonvolatile ways to generate regular income, often free of federal income tax and sometimes free of your state taxes as well.

CHAPTER 7

Money Every Month

Earning Income

Most of us have spent the greater part of our adult lives seeking and earning income. Many of us began the quest for income well before adulthood. I started when I was about 8 years old, pulling weeds for my mom and dad in the garden. Before I got to high school, I earned income mowing lawns, cleaning stalls, throwing hay bales, and doing general farm work.

No matter when you began, chances are you have spent a great deal of your life earning income. You may have been involved in a manufacturing process, sold real estate, practiced law or medicine, reported for a newspaper, delivered packages, or driven a rig over the road, but the fact is that you have made money through the use of your time. You may very well have enjoyed what you were doing, but for the vast majority, it was also done out of necessity. Unless you were born with a silver spoon in your mouth and have not spit it out, the fact is that you (like almost everyone else) need income.

In this chapter, we investigate a method of generating regular income at a fairly high rate. We explore how to make this money without the necessity of devoting the enormous time and effort we have devoted to our jobs and careers. We will see how this delightful result can be accomplished with relatively little effort and with modest risk at worst. Sometimes we can even enjoy the income free of federal income tax and, depending on the investment, free of state income tax as well.

One investment vehicle I use to generate regular monthly income is the closed-end fund. Before explaining the benefits and uses of the closed-end fund, I want to explain the differences between an open-end and a closed-end fund.

OPEN-END VS. CLOSED-END FUNDS

At the outset, let me be clear that I do not like open-end mutual funds. I believe there are much better ways to invest one's money without incurring what I believe are the very high charges made by these funds. In Chapter 8, we explore one positive alternative in detail, but, for now, I just want to define the major differences between open- and closed-end funds.

Open-End Funds, aka Mutual Funds

Investment companies operate open-end funds by raising money from shareholders who have the opportunity to buy or sell shares at the net asset value (NAV) each day. These are what we most commonly know as mutual funds. Money is raised continually by selling shares to the public, and that money is used to buy investments and pay the investment company management and associated fees. Investments must be made in accordance with a set of stated objectives, and any given fund is not permitted to deviate from those objectives. These funds consistently redeem and sell shares, so there is no fixed number of shares. The number of shares fluctuates as they are sold or redeemed. The public can continue to buy shares as long as the fund allows, and, of course, shares can be redeemed (sold by the shareholders). Cash always must be kept on hand in these funds, so they can pay shareholders who are redeeming their shares.

Often, these open-end funds also require a minimum investment. While one of the selling points of open-end funds is that they are professionally managed, I am not overly enthralled with the success of such professional management. No one cares as much about your money as you do, including the professional money manager. If we look at the performance of many open-end funds as the markets were crashing in 2000, we would have to conclude that many did not do a particularly good job in protecting shareholder investments or in cutting losses. Many of the funds that had been continuing to tout the upside joined the stampede when the market turned over.

The professional management also comes at quite a high cost. A couple of years ago, my wife and I were visiting an upscale resort and playing golf on the island of Maui. One day, on the golf course, we were paired with a pleasant young man who told us he was vacationing for several weeks with his wife, children, mother-in-law, and nanny. Since the resort was exquisite and quite expensive, as was the golf, I was curious how this young family could afford such an extravagant vacation. It turned out that the fellow was the manager of a poorly performing open-end mutual fund. As the NAV of the fund dwindled, he was being paid a fortune for his "professional management." In fact, during our short association, he was doing no fund management whatsoever. In this case, the shareholders were paying high fees and getting a poor return with a highly paid manager who was attending to his golf game rather than to business.

I do not mean to suggest that strong, competent fund managers should not be well paid; they should. I also doubt that most professional money managers are as cavalier about their failures as my young golfing friend. My complaint is that failures to perform well should not be highly rewarded at the expense of the shareholders who have entrusted their money to professional management. One of the ways around this predicament for the investor is to gain some knowledge yourself, as you are doing now. Then you can at least watch your own money intelligently. My wife and I were able to enjoy Maui from the fruits of our own investments. We refused to place our trust in the highly paid and only sometimes successful professional money managers, since we knew that our money would never be as important to them as it was to us.

Closed-End Funds Trade Like Stocks

Closed-end funds differ from open-end funds in that the closed-end funds sell a fixed number of shares in an original offering and are, thereafter, traded just like stocks on an exchange. Since they are traded like stocks, there is no minimum investment, and the price is based on the market rather than on the NAV. Closed-end funds can trade at a discount or premium to the NAV. Since there are a fixed number of shares, the closed-end funds do not have to keep cash on hand to redeem shares as the open-end funds must. As a result, the closed-end funds can be fully invested at all times. Closed-end fund managers do not have to worry about money flowing into or out of the fund from new purchases or redemptions, so they can concentrate more readily on the investments. Of course, these managers, too, are paid high fees for their services.

I recently checked an annual report for some closed-end insured municipal bond funds to check out the general level of fees charged. One fund I examined charged an "investment adviser fee" of more than $10 million on income of a little over $76 million. That's a charge of about 13.5 percent of the income. In addition, there was a "custodian fee" of nearly $700,000 plus legal fees, trustees' fees, and so on. These fees and expenses were generated to trade *insured municipal bonds*. In fairness to that fund, for the first five years, roughly half the fees were refunded, so, overall, about

7 percent was being charged to trade very safe and easily found issues. Of course, after five years, half the fees are no longer reimbursed and the fees actually paid go up. Whenever buying these funds, it is important to be aware of the charges incurred and to realize that most of the time the charges are made whether a fund is doing well or not.

Funds offer a wide variety of opportunities, from municipal bonds to emerging markets and everything in between. Technically, closed-end funds include the increasingly popular exchange-traded funds (ETFs), and I will devote all of Chapter 8 to them. I should note that the ETFs generally do not incorporate as hefty a fee as many of the other funds.

TRADING CLOSED-END FUNDS FOR TAX-FREE INCOME

In spite of the charges assessed by closed-end funds, I do like to trade many of them for income. As I mentioned earlier, the closed-end funds trade like stock, so they can be bought and sold on the open market. Naturally, commissions are charged on those transactions. There are times when some of these funds can be bought at a discount to their NAV, and that ability can lead to some handsome reward-to-risk ratios. Since income is important to most of us, including me, I frequently invest in closed-end funds that pay dividends on a monthly basis.

As I proceed with an explanation of some of the fantastic benefits of trading certain closed-end funds, particularly tax advantages, I must hasten to point out that I do not pretend to be a tax expert and I urge you to consult a competent tax adviser (one who is familiar with trading) before leaping into any of these positions for tax benefits. Really, talk to a tax adviser. The money you spend will be worth it. Get the advice first, then act; do not act, then try to find someone to fix your mistakes. Ready, fire, aim is a bad way to shoot and a terrible way to trade.

Although I do not pretend to be a tax expert, let me say that some closed-end funds are specifically designed to provide federally tax-free income. Those funds are often managed by reputable firms and limit their investments to tax-free municipal bonds. I have invested in federally tax-free funds managed by Alliance, Blackrock, Dreyfus, Evergreen, Eaton Vance, Morgan Stanley, Nuveen, and Sun Life Financial, to name a few. That list is not meant to be either a recommendation or exhaustive, but should serve to demonstrate that some of the very well-known investment companies are involved in offering federally tax-free closed-end municipal bond funds.

Based on my entry price, I have regularly found funds paying 5.5 percent or better annually and are federally tax free as well. Quite often, the dividends are paid on a monthly basis.

A number of these funds are also insured, so risk is significantly reduced. The yield on the insured funds tends to be a bit less, but the coverage insures payment of both interest and repayment of the bonds' principal, so a slightly lesser return may suit many investors. While writing this chapter, I checked out several insured and uninsured municipal funds managed by a number of different companies. The insured funds were yielding 4.8 to 5 percent annually (paid monthly) and the uninsured funds were yielding from about 5.2 to 5.5 percent. Overall, though there are occasional defaults by municipalities, municipal bonds tend to be relatively safe. As part of an investor's plan, she should decide whether she would require only insured funds or would also accept uninsured funds and, if so, what mix would be appropriate for her individual circumstances.

We have already seen that federally tax-free funds are available and that insured funds can also be purchased. In addition, some funds are what are known as "double tax free." In other words, they are free of both federal and state tax. Some funds are targeted to residents of highly populated states or states where there is a concentration of wealth such as Arizona, California, Florida, Maryland, Massachusetts, Minnesota, New Jersey, New York, Ohio, Pennsylvania, and Virginia. These funds invest in municipal bonds in the individual states in order to attempt to provide income free of both federal and state taxes. Indeed, even some of the double-tax-free funds are insured as well. A partial listing of federal tax-free, double-tax-free, and insured closed-end municipal funds can be found in Appendix B.

Commonly, I have found that these tax-free closed-end funds are not terribly expensive and can be found in a range of around $5 or $6 to perhaps $20 or so a share. Since the share price is related to interest rates, they also do not seem to be particularly volatile. Often, they seem to channel up and down within a range, and that type of movement can also provide an opportunity to trade on the price movement as well as to enjoy the regular monthly income. I keep a watch list of 30 or 40 of these tax-free funds and buy when I see one bouncing off a support or an uptrend line. I hold them until they turn down from a resistance or break down through a support, and as soon as I sell one issue, I review the watch list for another that is turning up from a support. In that way, I almost always have one or more positions that are rising and providing income at the same time. It has been surprising to me to realize that whenever I am exiting a down-turning position, I almost invariably will find another that is coming up off a support.

As an example, I bought Blackrock Municipal Income Trust (BFK) for $17.35 a share in December. It was paying $0.08 a share per month or an annual rate of 5.5 percent free of federal tax. I kept the fund for two dividend payments and then sold it for $17.83 as it began a dip. In less than two months, I realized $0.16 a share in tax-free income and made a profit of $0.48 a share on the sale of my position. That is a total return of $0.64, or about 3.7 percent, in about 45 days. If I am able to do that all year long, I can realize an annual return of around 30 percent. In another instance, I bought shares of Colonial High Income Municipal Trust (CXE) for $6.43 a share. That fund was paying $0.03 a share per month, or an annual dividend of 5.6 percent (federally tax free) on my investment. I sold these shares about three months later for $6.62. I had collected $0.09 a share in dividend and made another $0.19 a share, for a total return of about 4.4 percent in fewer than three months on my investment. While it may not make your hair stand on end, 4 percent a quarter, a portion of which is tax free, is considered to be a decent return in some circles, particularly when trading relatively low volatility issues.

You should be aware that many of these issues do not trade heavily, and often average volume of less than 100,000 shares a day, sometimes much less. Since liquidity can be a concern, I never take very large positions in any specific fund. For example, if a fund averages 50,000 or 75,000 shares a day traded, I rarely will take a position greater than about 2 percent of the average daily volume. If the fund trades 10,000 or 15,000 shares a day, I never take a position in excess of 500 shares. If the fund is trading fewer than 10,000 shares a day, I generally stay away and look for one with a bit more liquidity. If the price turns against me, I want to be able to exit the position without concerns about liquidity.

Figure 7.1 includes the charts of four separate closed-end funds (ARK, MPT, BKK, and APX). I selected them randomly to show a couple of different things. First, you can see that the price did not vary too significantly. ARK only moved between about $6 and $6.50 a share through the first three months of 2007. MPT channeled between about $13 and $13.50, while BKK also had about a $0.50 range during the period. APX was the biggest mover and only ranged about $0.60. It is also apparent on the right sides of the charts that, as one turned down (e.g., APX), another simultaneously was providing an entry on an upturn (MPT).

By employing the methodology of exiting on a downturn and looking for another fund that is turning up off support, I am almost always able to have positions in at least a couple of these funds. Often, I am able to realize decent gains on the price move as well as reaping the benefits of the interest income. Of course, any capital gain captured on the sale will be a taxable gain; it is only the interest that may be free of tax.

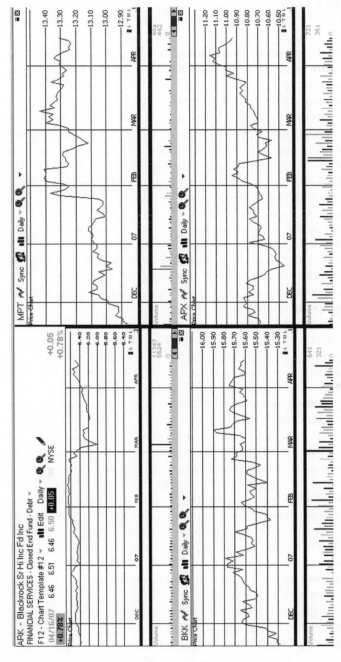

FIGURE 7.1 Comparison of Closed-End Charts. (Telechart 2005® chart courtesy of Worden Brothers, Inc.)

TAXABLE INCOME STREAMS FROM CLOSED-END FUNDS

According to statistics compiled by the Investment Company Institute (ICI), more than half of closed-end funds in 2003 were domestic municipal bond funds. In addition to those tax-free municipal bond funds, there are now a myriad of closed-end funds available whose objective is to provide a high level of current income. Though the income is taxable, some of those investments offer very attractive returns. In my estimation, there is nothing wrong with paying taxes as long as the net return is good. Some of these are diversified funds that invest in many different stocks or bonds, while others are nondiversified and limit their area of investment relatively strictly. Since the income generated by many of these funds is taxable, the before-tax rate of return is often higher than that realized by the tax-free funds.

Following is a discussion of specific funds and the manner in which they were investing in order to attempt to provide fairly high levels of income at the time I wrote this chapter. As you read this information, be aware that changes in prices, yields, returns, and investment strategies may have taken place in any or all of these specific funds and you will need to investigate them yourself and at the current time before considering or making any investment in any of them.

Some of the nondiversified closed-end funds may seek to provide a high level of current income by investing mainly in the senior debt of companies. As of the time of this writing, Blackrock Senior High Income Fund (ARK) was an example of just such a fund. It was trading around $6.40 a share and paying a monthly dividend of about 4.7 cents a share a month or 56 cents a share per year, for an annual yield of almost 8.8 percent. Just as with the case of the closed-end municipal bond funds, ARK trades like a stock, so the price would be expected to fluctuate up and down, giving the investor the opportunity to sell the shares for a profit (or a loss) as well. Another example of a fund that invests in high-yield debt securities is Evergreen Income Advantage Fund (EAD). At this writing, however, EAD was a diversified fund that invested the bulk of its money in loans and preferred stock as well as the high-yield debt securities. It was yielding nearly 10 percent a year with a share price just north of $14.

Recall the "buy/write" strategy discussed in Chapter 5. That is the strategy where the investor buys a stock and, at the same time writes (sells) a covered call on the stock. The strategy has an advantage of bringing in income and reducing risk in the stock. Risk, of course, remains and is equivalent to the purchase price of the stock less the amount received from writing the call. Some closed-end funds such as the Eaton Vance Tax-Managed Buy Write Income Fund (ETB) employed essentially that strategy. As of this writing, Eaton Vance was yielding about 8.5 percent annually and was selling at a share price near $21. In this instance, the shareholder has professional management executing the strategy on her behalf. ING Global Equity Dividend & Premium and Opportunity Fund (IGD) and ING Global Advantage & Premium Fund (IGA) were utilizing somewhat similar strategies except that they were investing in global common stocks with dividend histories and option writing strategies. Each of those funds was also paying dividends in the 8 to 9 percent annual range on a monthly basis. Other investment companies like Nuveen have funds using similar strategies.

Some funds even employ collars in an attempt to garner strong total return through current income, capital gains, and capital appreciation. One of these, ING Risk Managed Natural Resource Fund (IRR) was doing exactly that with investments in the natural resources and energy industries. In Chapter 6, we discussed the enhanced safety a collar could provide in exchange for a somewhat limited upside. Presumably, that is the desired goal for funds that incorporate collar strategies into their investments.

Other closed-end funds may emphasize consistent long-term levels of return. One such fund is the Gabelli Global Utility (GLU) which invests mainly in the utility industry with emphasis on dividends. As we see funds like this one that focus on sectors, we are getting closer to the exchange-traded fund, which is the subject of Chapter 8.

SUMMARY

There certainly is no lack of diversity in closed-end funds. There are as many designs to produce income as the mind can conjure. The investor needs to examine the methods and results of the many offerings to find a fit with her own goals and risk tolerances. Vehicles from insured double-tax-free municipal bond funds to riskier emerging market funds are out there. You need to see which of them, if any, fit your personal business plan.

In this chapter, we distinguished open from closed-end funds and looked at the relatively high costs associated with the ownership of mutual funds. Though I am not a big fan of mutual funds in general, I make some exceptions, particularly with regard to closed-end municipal bond funds. Those funds can provide a regular stream of income free of federal tax and, depending on the fund, sometimes also free of state taxes. The yields can be attractive, and, if the investor seeks even greater security by giving up a little on the yield side, insured funds can be utilized as well. Since these closed-end funds also trade like a stock, the investor can trade for price appreciation as well as for income stream. I sometimes exit positions in these funds when the price turns down and immediately enter another fund with a similar yield that appears to be turning up. In that way, I can benefit both from the income return and also from the price appreciation.

Chapter 8 discusses ETFs, which are technically closed-end funds but generally are subject to lesser management fees. They provide an increasingly popular and often fantastic vehicle for the investor.

Getting an Edge with Exchange-Traded Funds

I t's important to look for every advantage when trading. Trading stocks subjects you not only to the general risks of the market, but also to the individual risks of the company we are trading. Every company runs the risk of having a bad year, introducing a product that fails, losing market share to new competition, facing a lawsuit, suffering a CEO who commits some major (or minor) publicized transgression, and on and on.

I have always suggested that a trader searching for an entry into any position first check the markets. If the markets are bullish, that can be a pretty good reason to look for a bullish play. Next, find a sector that is bullish in the bullish market, and, finally, find a stock that looks bullish in the bullish sector. By doing that we have taken steps to try to give ourselves an edge by choosing a position where, at that moment, everything is at least pointed in the same direction. Having accomplished that much, if we are buying a single stock, we are still faced with the dangers inherent in investment in a single company. If we could buy a whole market, or even a sector, we could reduce the risks of single-stock ownership and, in my view, have an easier time making our selections.

Exchange-traded funds, or ETFs, provide us with precisely that opportunity. They are vehicles that can help us reduce the risks of individual stock ownership and, at the same time, provide most, if not all, of the benefits of owning equities.

WHAT ARE ETFS?

ETFs are closed-end funds, or a basket of stocks traded as a single stock. The basket may contain many or few stocks, but the trader normally knows exactly what is in each basket at any given time. ETFs have been around since the early 1990s, but have surged in popularity in more recent years.

I wonder why investors even bother buying open-end mutual funds any longer when I consider the positive advantages of many ETFs. I suppose open-end funds are still popular at least in part because of their professional management, but I suspect that they will lose favor with even the modestly sophisticated investor as more people learn about the advantages offered by ETFs.

ADVANTAGES OF ETFS

ETFs have many positive characteristics and incorporate a multitude of advantages for the investor. This chapter covers a number of the benefits presented to the ETF investor and includes the following:

- Ability to trade whole markets.
- Ability to trade complete sectors.
- Ability to trade specific styles (e.g., large-cap, mid-cap, value, etc.).
- Ability to trade foreign equities.
- Ability to trade commodities.
- Ability to trade real estate.
- Ability to trade bonds.
- Relative ease of trading.
- Relative low cost.
- Ability to trade options on the ETFs.
- Content of ETFs is transparent—you know exactly what you are trading.
- ETFs are tax efficient.
- ETFs enable easy diversification.

Trading a Basket

In my view, one of the major benefits of ETFs is that they enable the investor to trade a basket of stocks, bonds, styles, or foreign nation stocks like a single stock without the risk of single-stock ownership. Unlike a rotten apple, one bad stock does not necessarily spoil the whole ETF basket.

For example, if we are trading a basket filled with all the Dow 30 Industrials as the Diamonds Trust Series (DIA) ETF and one Dow component has some bad news, the stock with the bad news may suffer a very serious tumble, but, in all probability, the DIA will not drop nearly as significantly as the affected stock. In fact, the DIA could even move up if the other Dow components are doing well and the bad news is specific to the stricken stock.

I mentioned earlier that determining the direction of a whole market is easier than determining the direction of a specific stock. ETFs, among other things, permit us to trade a whole market as a single stock. iShares™, for example, offers some very broad market ETFs such as the S&P 1500 Index Fund (ISI); the NYSE Composite Fund (NYC), which seeks results (before fees and expenses) that correspond to the price and yield performance of the NYSE Composite Index; and the Russell 3000 Index Fund (IWV). Perhaps the most popular of all the broader market ETFs is the "Qs." The "Qs" is slang for the Nasdaq 100 Index Tracking Stock ETF with the trading symbol QQQQ. On an average day, the "Qs" trades upward of 120 million shares, so liquidity is definitely not a concern. This ETF enables the investor to hold a basket of stocks that generally correspond to the price and yield performance of the Nasdaq 100 Index®. Now, the investor can trade essentially the whole Nasdaq 100 in one ETF rather than having to buy or sell 100 separate stocks.

Just as one can trade the whole Nasdaq 100 with the Qs, one can also trade the whole S&P 500 with the "Spiders," which is slang for SPDR (Standard and Poor's Depositary Receipts). SPY is the symbol for the SPDR S&P 500 Trust Series ETF. By utilizing SPY, the investor is able to emulate the performance of the whole S&P 500. I often have positions in both the Qs and SPY, since they represent large and important market segments. Though we usually hear the news commentators dwelling on the performance of the Dow Industrials, I believe the S&P 500, the Nasdaq 100, and the NYSE Composite Index paint a more accurate picture of the whole market because of their significantly broader base. The Dow Industrials include only 30 stocks, and though they are important companies, they are only a small part of a stock market that includes nearly 7,000 listed issues.

Sector Rotation

In addition, to encompassing broad market segments, many ETFs are designed to track various sectors of the market. There is a theory of sector rotation that hypothesizes that most of the money stays in the market but moves from sector to sector as one sector loses favor and another gains popularity. Whether the theory is completely correct or not may be immaterial, but it is clear that different sectors perform better at different times.

Therefore, the ability to move money into a strengthening sector and out of a weakening sector can be quite advantageous.

One device that is available to invest in individual sectors is the Select Sector SPDR. These "spiders" divide the market into nine sectors: consumer discretionary (XLY), consumer staples (XLP), energy (XLE), financial (XLF), health care (XLV), industrial (XLI), materials (XLB), technology (XLK), and utilities (XLU). The consumer discretionary SPDR ETF, for example, includes stocks in various companies in the automotive, consumer durables, apparel, retail, hotel, restaurant, and leisure categories. You can find the categories included in each of these Select Sector SPDRs as well as the companies held by going to the web site at www.spdrindex.com and choosing the sector that interests you.

iShares™ also offers a large variety of sector ETFs, including Dow Jones U.S. Broker-Dealers (IAI), Dow Jones U.S. Insurance Index (IAK), Dow Jones U.S. Regional Banks (IAT), Nasdaq Biotechnology Index Fund (IBB), Goldman Sachs Natural Resources Fund (IGE), Goldman Sachs Software Index Fund (IGV), and Goldman Sachs Semiconductor Fund (IGW), to name but a few of many.

Another variant of the basket concept are the Holding Company Depositary Receipts (HOLDRs), which own selected companies in a particular industry, sector, or group. Unlike an ETF, HOLDRs do not track an underlying index but represent a piece of an industry. The content of each HOLDR is determined by Merrill Lynch, which also decides the weighting. An example of a HOLDR is the Biotech HOLDR (BBH), which has a majority of its assets invested in Amgen (AMGN) and Genentech (DNA). Another example of a HOLDR is the B2B Internet (BHH). HOLDRs also differ from the standard ETF in that they can only be bought and sold in round lots of 100.

Invest in Styles of Stock

ETFs also provide the ability to invest in styles of stocks such as large-cap, large-cap growth, small-cap value, and almost anything in between. You name it and you can probably find it. For example, you could choose the Morningstar Small Value (JKL) or the Morningstar Mid Value (JKI) or the Morningstar Large Value Index Funds (JKF). If you prefer to focus on growth in an ETF, you could look to the same Morningstar series of Small (JKK), Mid (JKH), or Large Growth (JKE) Index Funds. Many times, growth stocks will be faring better than value in the marketplace so you have the opportunity to choose an ETF to go with the current flow and then can switch when the market adjusts from growth to value.

Foreign Equities

ETFs also enable us to invest in international and country-specific equities as well. The iShares™ MSCI Japan Index Fund ETF (EWJ) jumped almost 250 percent from its low in 2003 to its high in May 2006. China has recently been a hot area for investment and ETF opportunities exist there as well. Since its inception in 2004, the iShares™ FTSE/Xinhau China 25 Index Fund ETF (FXI) has soared with only the occasional retracement. With some exceptions, you can find an ETF for almost any country that interests you. Brazil, for example, is available through the iShares™ MSCI Brazil Index Fund ETF (EWZ). If you have any doubt about the popularity of some of these funds, EWZ has had average volume over 3 million shares a day over the last many months as I write this section. Index Funds (ETFs) are currently available for at least Australia (EWA), Canada (EWC), Sweden (EWD), Germany (EWG), Hong Kong (EWH), Italy (EWI), Belgium (EWK), Switzerland (EWL), Malaysia (EWM), the Netherlands (EWN), Austria (EWO), Spain (EWP), France (EWQ), Singapore (EWS), Taiwan (EWT), the United Kingdom (EWU), and Mexico (EWW).

At times, emerging markets provide very rapid growth. If emerging markets interest you, there are ETFs that provide an investment vehicle for them. Sponsored by Nasdaq Global Funds, Inc., the Baskets of Listed Depositary Receipts (BLDRs) Emerging Markets 50 ADR Index Fund (ADRE) is designed to generally correspond to the price and dividend yield performance (before fees and expenses) of the Bank of New York Emerging Markets 50 ADR Index. While daily volume traded in this fund is not nearly as large as that of the Brazil fund (EWZ) alluded to earlier, I believe it is sufficiently liquid, at a current average of over 175,000 shares a day, to take at least small positions (1,000 shares or less) when the investor finds good entries and a nearby exit in the event of a quick reversal.

Commodities

A complete index of commodities can be traded using the Powershares DB Commodity Index Tracking Fund (DBC). Certain individual commodities such as precious metals can also be traded using ETFs. Gold, for example, can be traded through Street Tracks Gold Trust (GLD), the sole assets of which are gold bullion and, at times, cash. For some, an investment in this ETF may present a more convenient method of investing in gold than buying gold itself and facing issues of storage and insurance. Trading in GLD has also been quite liquid, so issues related to buying and selling may not be as cumbersome as buying coin or bars might have been in the past. Trading is also possible in silver utilizing iShares® Silver Trust (SLV).

With the ever-increasing popularity of ETFs, it would not be surprising to see new ETFs for various commodities in the future.

Real Estate Investment Trusts

Almost every investor should consider including real estate in his portfolio. Some of the greatest fortunes in history have resulted from real estate investments. In modern times, few are better known than Donald Trump, who has become both rich and famous through his insightful acumen in the real estate world. Most of us do not have the knowledge, time, energy, or capital to operate at Trump's level, but we do have the ability to invest some of our capital in real estate without taking on the management obligations inherent in personal real estate ownership.

Real estate investment trusts (REITs) are companies that purchase and/or manage real estate using money invested by shareholders. They are obligated by law to distribute 90 percent of their taxable income to the shareholders, so they often are excellent sources of income. The investor has a wide array of choices since there are many REITs in a variety of segments of the real estate market including office, health care, industrial, retail, hotel/motel, apartments, residential, or geographical region.

While not ETFs, REITs do have a number of positive characteristics in addition to providing income and enabling the investor to enter broad-based segments of the real estate market with relatively little capital. They often also offer a low beta (low volatility compared to the market as a whole), high returns, and growth potential. Like ETFs, REITs trade like stocks, so they are generally quite liquid and permit relative ease of entry and exit that would not be available to the real estate owner. Care should be taken to assure that any given REIT trades enough average daily volume to satisfy the needs of the individual investor.

While not all REITs are ETFs, there are ETF REITs. An example is the Vanguard REIT ETF (VNQ).

As with almost any investment, risks do exist. Some of the risks inherent in investment in REITs result from real estate cycles, management weaknesses, aging properties, and size and management of debt.

Bonds

The investor can even use ETFs to take a position in government bonds. I sometimes invest in shares of the iShares™ Lehman 20+ Year Treasury Bond Fund ETF (TLT) both for the regular monthly interest payments and the possible price appreciation. Other terms such as the 7–10 Year Treasury Bonds (IEF) are also available.

Costs

I have already set out my objections to open-end and some closed-end mutual funds because of the high costs associated with ownership in the form of management and miscellaneous fees. ETFs have a significant advantage over open-end mutual funds in the expense ratio category. Since the ETFs are normally based on indexes and therefore do not have to be actively managed, the fees are ordinarily much less. If there is such a thing as "passive" management, that is what we would expect to occur with index funds. The fund manager only needs to follow a fixed index of securities, so one would expect less trading in the fund than in an open-end mutual fund.

The trader or investor should be aware that brokerage commissions will be charged when buying and selling ETFs since they trade like stock, and, of course, gains and losses will ordinarily have tax consequences just as they do when trading stocks.

Based on expense ratios alone, my choice would almost always be to buy an ETF for a sector rather than an open-end mutual fund designed to trade the same sector. Since stocks in a sector often tend to move together, I believe that the costly professional management of an open-end sector fund would require a significantly greater return just to equal the performance of a less expense-burdened ETF trading the index of the same sector.

Trading

ETFs are just great to trade. They do not carry the risk of the individual stock, yet they can be traded in exactly the same fashion. ETFs can be traded throughout the day just like any stock and are not redeemed at the end-of-day net asset value (NAV) like open-end mutual funds. Since they are traded like stocks, their price is dependent on supply and demand, and they can trade above or below the NAV. You are also able to get a current quote at any time either from your broker or from a real-time service if you have access to one. There is no minimum investment, and generally there is no requirement that round lots (in increments of 100 shares) be purchased or sold.

ETFs also can be sold short, giving the trader the opportunity to profit on a downward move of a market or index. Unlike a stock, they can even be sold short on a downtick. In addition to the ability to short an ETF, there are actually ETFs that play the short side of the market. The ProShares Short QQQ ETF (PSQ), for example, is the equivalent of shorting the QQQQ. As QQQQ goes down in price, PSQ goes up. Some ETFs even double the movement. ProShares UltraShort Dow30 (DXD) seeks results (after fees and expenses) that correspond to twice the opposite of the Dow 30's daily performance.

One relatively simple strategy I have employed with QQQQ is to enter the ETF when the 15-day exponential moving average crosses above the 30-day exponential moving average. I remain in the position as long as the 15-day average stays above the 30. When the 15 crosses below the 30, I sell the stock I own and can then short the stock. If I am short the stock, I wait until the 15-day moving average crosses back above the 30-day, and then I buy to cover my short position. Since the 15-day average is now above the 30-day again, I can repeat the process. In that fashion, I am profiting whether the market is moving up or down just as long as the "Q's" stay in a trend in one direction or the other. As with the use of any moving average crossover strategy, there is the danger or being whipsawed if the ETF (or stock) stops trending and begins to trade in a tight channel. If that occurs, I simply abandon the play and wait for a trend to become established again. You do not need to confine yourself to the 15- and 30-day averages, but can experiment with paper trades on any two time frames to see what works best for you and your personal trading style.

Figure 8.1 illustrates the potential entries and exits utilizing the 15- and 30-day moving average crossovers. The price graph is represented by the solid black line and the 15-day moving average by the gray dashed line. The 30-day moving average is represented by the black dashed line. You can see where I have noted three instances where the 15-day moving average crossed over the 30-day, which could have served as bullish entries. I also noted one place (in the middle of the chart) where the 15-day crossed below the 30, which could have served as a bearish entry. In each instance where I placed notes, you can see that there was a potential for great profit just using these entries. It is also important to see that there would have been some whipsawing where the price ran sideways. When a sideways

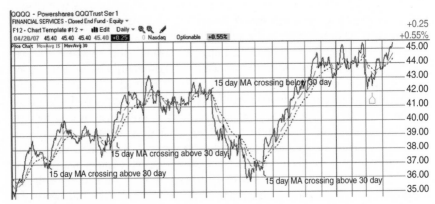

FIGURE 8.1 Moving Average Crossovers. (Telechart 2005® chart courtesy of Worden Brothers, Inc.)

movement is occurring, the moving average crossover method of entering and exiting can result in getting into and out of a position several times for small gains or small losses, but also incurring commissions each time a trade is made. However, in my experience, the large moves more than make up for the whipsaws.

The investor is able to place stop loss, stop limit, contingent stop, trailing stop, and limit orders on ETFs, which is a tremendous plus. I travel quite a bit and often leave with a number of positions in place. When I have an ETF that is already in a profitable position, I regularly place a percentage trailing stop, good 'til canceled; that way, no matter where I am or what I am doing, I remain in the position as long as it is going in my direction, or at least is not reversing more than the percentage I have allowed.

Suppose, for example, that I bought 1,000 shares of QQQQ at $40 as the Nasdaq is moving up and that I am getting ready to embark on a cruise to South America. The ETF has moved to $42 before I leave and the markets still look strong. I am going to be out of touch for quite a while. What do I do? I could simply close the position and take my $2 profit, but I would much rather try to benefit from additional upward movement. In that case, I could place a trailing stop loss based on a percentage. Let us say that I was willing to risk a 2 percent move down from $42. If QQQQ dropped 2 percent or $0.84, it would be at $41.16 and I would still be up $1.16 from my original purchase. I would place a 2 percent trailing stop order, good 'til canceled. What happens from there is that as the ETF reaches new highs, my trailing order moves up with it. Initially, with the Qs at $42, a reduction of 2 percent from that price to $41.16 would trigger the sale, but as the stock rises, so too does the stop. If the Qs reached $44 as I was sailing along, the stop would still trail by 2 percent, but now, using $44, a 2 percent drop would take me out if the stock dipped to $43.12. Unless it dipped that low, I would still be in the position. As the stock climbs, my exit climbs with it. Only if it turns down 2 percent from the most recent high am I taken out, so I can sail blissfully along, letting the ETF help pay for my trip.

Trailing stops using "points" can also be set. Instead of using a percentage, I could use a dollar amount. Again, if the ETF were at $42 and I placed a trailing stop at $0.75, I would be taken out if the Qs dropped to $41.25. As the ETF climbed to $44, the stop would behit only if the price dropped back to $43.25. I personally prefer percentage trailing stops, but it truly is a matter of personal preference only.

A number of brokers permit the use of trailing stops and many do not have the ability to provide them. Since trailing stops can be quite helpful, particularly at times when you cannot be attentive to the market, check to see whether your broker offers that type of order If not, you may consider seeking out a brokerage where they are available.

In my view, the ability to use limit orders and stop orders gives ETFs a monumental advantage over open-end funds.

Though I am not a big fan of margin, as I mentioned early on, I do want to note that ETFs can be purchased on margin. As is the case with buying stock, margin can be wonderful if the position moves in the direction you want, but it can be very unpleasant if the position moves the wrong way. Just remember, when the broker is loaning you money to buy ETFs (or stock), all of the risk is yours and none of the risk is on the broker. The broker simply earns interest on the money loaned; you must repay the loan no matter what happens to the price of your investment.

Dividends

Depending on what ETF is chosen, the basket of securities may also pay dividends. A bond fund can almost certainly be expected to pay regular dividends. TLT (the iShares™ Lehman 20+ Years Treasury Bond Fund) is an example of an ETF that is invested in Treasury bonds and pays regular monthly dividends. The Diamonds (DIA), which track the Dow Industrials, also pay dividends based on the dividends paid by the Dow Industrial companies. These dividends are distributed to the shareholders, less expenses, on a pro rata basis. Naturally, the investor would expect some ETFs—a bond ETF or maybe a REIT ETF such as the Vanguard REIT ETF (VNQ)—to be a source of dividends. There is even a SPDR Dividends ETF (SDY), which is designed to correspond, after expenses, to the S&P High Yield Dividend Aristocrats Index.

However, some ETFs would be quite unlikely to pay dividends based on their past history. While there is no way to tell without checking the specific ETF, one might guess that a micro-cap ETF may be less likely to pay large dividends than a utility ETF. While seeking price appreciation in buying an ETF, it does not hurt to be on the receiving end of some dividends as well.

Option Availability

One of the benefits I enjoy about many of the ETFs is that they also have options. As I set out in Chapters 4, 5, and 6, there are a variety of ways to trade options, and with the availability of options on many ETFs, we can now apply many of those strategies to trading whole markets, sectors, foreign equities, some commodities, and even bonds.

Before trading options on any specific ETF, always make sure to check the open interest on the contract(s) you are considering. ETFs like the Qs or the Diamonds (DIA) or SPY will generally have plenty of open interest to assure sufficient liquidity, but some ETFs may not yet have enough open interest in at least some of their series to make a prudent investment. In checking for open interest as I write this section, for example, I found that while IWZ (iShares™ Russell 3000 Growth Index Fund) has options available, there was no open interest whatsoever for any strike of either puts or calls for the next eight months. Lack of open interest means lack of liquidity, and lack of liquidity means that you can be at the mercy of the market makers. That is a place you do not want to be. I suggest that you revisit your personal business plan and make sure that it includes a minimum open interest requirement before entering an option trade. I would never enter a pure option play unless the open interest on the specific contract (expiration and strike price of the put or call I am considering) is at least 100 contracts, and, generally, I stay away unless there is open interest of 300 contracts or more.

What fantastic possibilities option trading ETFs provide! We can now own an ETF that results in a broad market investment such as the S&P 500 (SPY), and we can sell covered calls each month against our position. Similarly, we can have a bullish broad market position and cover the possibility of a downturn with protective puts. We can make directional broad market or sector plays by buying calls if we are bullish or puts if we are bearish. We can generate income by creating spreads and we can even set up collars on broad market segments, sectors, foreign markets, or bond ETFs.

One strategy I often use with money that might be sitting idle is to buy shares of TLT (the iShares™ Lehman 20+ Years Treasury Bond Fund ETF) and place a collar. I buy the shares, buy some near-the-money protective puts, and sell some covered calls so that I bring in enough from the calls to at least pay for the protective puts and then enjoy the regular monthly income (about $0.50 a share per month) paid by the fund. When I can find the right collar, I have an income-producing position with no risk to the downside and some upside price potential as well.

Another positive for me is that the options on many of the heavily traded ETFs have strike prices that are only $1 apart instead of $2.50 or $5, as is the case with most stocks. QQQQ, DIA, SPY, IJR (iShares™) Small Cap 600 Index Fund), EWJ (iShares® MSCI Japan Index Fund), and the Select Sector SPDRs (XLB, XLF, XLK, XLP, XLI, XLU, XLV, and XLY), to name just a few, all offer strike prices that are only $1 apart. I really like to trade spreads when I can use legs that have a spread of only $1 since the dollar risk is generally so small. As an example, as I am writing this section, QQQQ is trading above a little support at $44. With about three weeks to go before expiration, I could sell the $44 puts for $0.55 and buy the $43s for $0.30 to take in $0.25 a share before commissions. If I were to sell 10 contracts of the $44 puts and buy 10 contracts of the $43 puts, before calculating the credit, I would have $1,000 at risk (10 contracts times 100 shares per contract times $44 if put to me, minus 10 contracts times 100 shares per contract times $43 if I in turn assigned the shares to someone else). However, since the market is giving me $250 (10 contracts times 100 shares per contract times $0.25), my risk is only $750. If I can make $250 on a $750 risk, I have a potential 33 percent return on risk (250 divided by 750) for a three-week play. Of course, if QQQQ is below $44 at expiration and I had done nothing to adjust, the shares would be put to me at $44, and I would in turn assign them to someone else at $43 for a $1,000 loss less the $250 the market paid me to enter the positions originally.

Transparency

Yet another advantage I see of ETFs over open-end mutual funds is transparency. Transparency simply means we know what we own at any given time. Unlike most mutual funds, we can precisely determine the holdings of most ETFs on any given day. For example, if we own iShares™, we need only go to the web site (www.ishares.com) and look at the holdings for any specific iShares™ ETF. Since most ETFs are based on indices, we can look at the given index to determine holdings. Open-end mutual funds often have ever-changing holdings as fund managers move in and out of positions, so it is much more difficult to ascertain what their holdings may be at any specific time.

Tax Efficiency

It is at least broadly true that any time a trade is made, there is a tax consequence. Short-term trades where the holding period is 12 months or less (and all short sales) are normally treated as short-term capital gains or short-term capital losses. The short-term gains are currently treated as ordinary income and taxed at regular income tax rates. Long-term trades are trades that last for more than 12 months, and long-term capital gains are generally taxed at a rate that is significantly less than the ordinary income tax rate (at least for now).

Open-end mutual funds are often managed fairly actively, and there can be a relatively high number of trades. When many trades are made, there can be many realized capital gains, each generating a tax consequence. Since ETFs are frequently tied to or based on an index, their holdings will remain relatively constant. Whatever is included in the index is what they are likely to hold and unless the composition of the index changes, the holdings in the ETF are likely to remain essentially the same. As a consequence, we would expect significantly less turnover in an ETF and, therefore, fewer realized capital gains that would be subject to taxation.

The investor should be aware that anytime she trades into or out of a fund, there is going to be a realized short- or long-term gain or loss, and those activities will result in tax consequences. Again, I confess no expertise in the tax arena and urge you to consult with a tax professional where your own trading and investing is concerned. It is my understanding, however, that short-term capital losses can be used to offset short-term capital gains, and long-term capital losses can be used to offset long-term capital gains.

Diversification

It seems obvious that ETFs enable an investor to diversify with great ease. The real question is: How can we benefit from the diversification that is possible with ETFs? We can hold a large part of the market just by purchasing shares of SPY, giving us a position in the S&P 500 stocks, or we can have a position in the stocks comprising the Nasdaq 100 Index by owning QQQQ. If diversification is the goal, it is easily done, but I do not believe that diversification in and of itself is the goal. The goal in trading or investing is to make money. If we own SPY and the market is falling, what is the point of the diversification? We would be diversified, but we would be losing money.

I believe that the value of diversification in ETFs is to significantly reduce the risk of single-stock ownership. Bad news about a single stock in the S&P 500 is unlikely to have too grave an effect on SPY, so ownership of that ETF and the resulting diversification insulates us somewhat from a serious decline in a single issue. The diversification, however, does not insulate us from a declining market. If the markets are trending upward, it is a good thing to own large segments such as those represented by SPY or QQQQ or DIA, but when the uptrend ends, it is time to leave those positions. The buy-and-hold crowd will argue that you should just hold on because the markets will come back. Maybe they will, but who can tell us when? If we see the uptrend is broken either because a trend line or an ascending moving average is broken, why not just exit. Take the profits and wait for the next turn up or sell the ETF short and make some money on the way down as well. I cannot understand holding a bullish position when I can see the value falling and falling. That is just stressful. Get out. When it turns back up, get back in and ride it up again, but do not lose sleep while a position loses more and more money.

Earlier in the chapter, we discussed sector rotation. If we buy an ETF that represents a sector, say health care, as it is going up, we have diversified our holdings within that sector. We could also hold several other sectors at the same time, further diversifying our overall holdings, but some of those sectors could be going down as others are going up. Why hold the ones that are going down? Diversification for the sake of diversification alone does not make sense. If we got into health care as it rose, let's get out when it turns down. Let's take that money and invest it in another sector that is rising. It is extremely rare to find all sectors falling at the same time, even if the overall markets are dropping. It takes little effort to find a sector that is rising and to ride it until it turns, and the rewards can be enormous. When that sector that was rising begins to fall, jump into another sector that is rising. Sometimes you may get whipsawed out when a sector makes a little "head fake," but lots of times you will be very happy with the results.

A WORD OF CAUTION ABOUT LIQUIDITY

I should caution the investor to check daily volume before jumping into any ETF. Some funds, like the DIA, Qs, or SPY, trade very large volume, but some of the more narrowly structured funds do not yet trade very many shares a day. I would suggest that you stay away from the lightly traded issues, since they can harbor some surprisingly unpleasant volatility. Instead, include an element in your business plan that requires a minimum average daily volume traded on an ETF before you consider taking a position in your own portfolio.

Personally, I stay away unless the ETF I am considering is trading an average of at least 250,000 shares a day. If I am trading options on ETFs, I try to restrict myself to trading those contracts that have at least 300 contracts of open interest, although, on very rare occasions, I would consider trading a small number of contracts (less than 10 percent of the open interest) if the open interest were between 100 and 300 contracts.

ETFs = SLICED BREAD?

While ETFs may not be the very best thing since sliced bread, they do provide some fantastic vehicles for the investor. They enable an investor to easily diversify and reduce volatility while enjoying the potential rewards of riding trends. ETFs have a reasonable cost structure that does not cut too deeply into potential returns. They are easily traded, and many offer the additional benefits of option trading to increase leverage or provide regular income. In short, it is no wonder that ETFs are becoming increasingly popular.

On the negative side, I see that the numbers of ETFs are increasing so dramatically and the contents of some of the baskets are becoming so specialized that the investor will need to be cautious to assure that the benefits of owning a basket are not lost. As the contents of the baskets of holdings decrease, the risk and volatility may well increase and the volume traded may become too little for safety.

In Appendix C, I have set out a number of categories and some of the ETFs and REITs traded in each as a ready reference to some of the more active funds that might provide investment vehicles to consider.

CHAPTER 9

What You Need to Get Started

This chapter covers essentials you need to become a successful investor or trader. We will look at the factors that should be considered when choosing a broker, including critical orders that are available through some brokerage firms (but not others) and examples of how they can be utilized. We will also explore the tools for trading and investing, including computer requirements and charting needs.

Every trader (at least, every *good* trader) is constantly expanding his knowledge about the markets and refining his approach to trading. We will review some of the choices for continuing education, and some ways to advance our trading knowledge and maintain discipline to ensure successful trading.

We will then add some additional information on the use and importance of volatility in trading some specific strategies.

This chapter ends with important "do's and don'ts" for trading, including my personal thoughts concerning successful trading.

CHOOSING A BROKER

To some, the broker is a necessary evil, but to others the broker can be a wonderful and trusted ally, teacher, adviser, and even friend. Admittedly, those in the latter categories seem to be very rare, indeed. If you are new to trading, learning new strategies, or simply lack experience, you will want to find the rarity—a great broker.

For many years, I have suggested that my option seminar students interview prospective brokers, by phone or in person, before signing on with any firm. I suggested that the students stay away from the large, well-known brokerage houses and contact the lesser-known medium and smaller-sized firms. In general, the big brokerages do not seem to want the option-oriented investor unless he comes equipped with a very significant bankroll. I do have one of my own accounts with a large, well-known firm because there is a broker there who is both knowledgeable and helpful.

A couple of years ago the branch I use promoted a new manager, and my broker invited me to lunch to meet the manager. As we began the conversation, the manager adeptly demonstrated that he knew nothing about nor cared anything about me or my trading even though I had a seven-figure account at his branch. He clearly was unaware that I regularly had referred seminar students to his firm. The manager started with the usual line about what good hands I was in with my broker and how the broker could lead me through the tortuous paths of "buy and hold." As a trial lawyer for many years, I have developed a nose for manure and his conversation was filled with the essence. Had it not been for my personal friendship with my broker, I would have left with my account before the hamburger arrived. Instead, I asked the pompous manager: "Exactly what kind of client are you seeking?" His expression was dumbfounded and unbelieving. "Why, we want all clients," he responded. I explained that I had referred a number of clients while the previous branch manager was in place and that many of my students were seeking a brokerage firm. Most, I explained, were just learning to trade options and did not have enough money to open accounts larger than $2,500 to $5,000. "Oh," he replied, "we're not really looking for options traders." "I see," I said. "I'm an options trader."

We went on to more mundane subjects and he left before coffee. I took a great deal of money away from my account at that firm and now use that account only for things like guaranteed annuities, the occasional stock purchase and covered call writing, and some closed-end funds. Though I still have a fairly large account there, I moved the bulk of my trading money to a firm more interested in and open to my style of trading as set out in my personal business plan.

My real point is that the brokerage is supposed to work for you, not dictate to you. Earlier, I mentioned interviewing prospective brokers before opening an account. If you are interested in trading options, when you call a firm, ask to speak with the broker who is the most active options trader in the firm. Shockingly, many brokers know very little about options trading. Sometimes they even may tell you that you should not trade options or that they would not allow options trading in your account. What? It is your account, is it not? Sometimes they tell you that you cannot trade options because, truth be told, their firm does not permit them to trade options. Options are too risky, they may say. What about a collar, you might ask. In any event, if the response to your inquiry is negative, move on to the next prospective broker.

When you do find someone who is willing to do what you want, ask them whether they trade options in their own account and, if so, what strategies they use. Ask them how successful they are with their option trades. Make sure they are going to be available throughout the market day or if they are not that someone else who knows what they are doing will be. That may sound a bit harsh, but remember, it was not long ago that many brokers were really little more than salespeople telling a story about stocks. A good broker will be knowledgeable and will be able and willing to teach you new strategies, countermeasures, and nuances of trading. Those rare brokers who both know and are willing to share are absolutely invaluable and literally can be worth their weight in gold. Make the effort (and it will be an effort) to find one, and the rewards will be great.

Once you are experienced, knowledgeable, and successful, you then may consider an online Internet broker. There is no reason to rush to these discount brokers simply because the commissions are so attractive compared to the so-called full-service broker. If you have found a good full-service broker (and I emphasize good), the difference in commissions may well be made up by things like good fills on your orders, good advice, and enhanced knowledge. I do not mean to disparage the online discount brokers. Many have excellent education on their sites and even conduct regular webinars to assist their clients. In the beginning, it may just be better to have someone you know and who will be responsive when you call.

I should explain a little about the importance of good fills. Suppose the April $40 options on ABC are quoted at $3.00 × $3.50. That means that someone is willing to pay $3 a share to buy the option and someone is willing to sell the option at $3.50 a share. The difference between the bid price and the ask price here is $0.50 and is known as the spread. If you want to buy 10 contracts of the ABC options, you know that you can get them for $3,500 (10 contracts times 100 shares per contract times $3.50) plus commission. If you placed a market order with an online discount broker where you are paying a $7.50 commission, that might be exactly what happens and you would wind up paying $3,507.50 for the filled order. However, if you have a broker who is really working for you, you might pay a $50 commission, but he may be able to get you a fill deep between the spread ($3 × $3.50). Suppose the broker can get your order filled at $3.30 instead of $3.50. Now your cost to enter the trade would be only $3,300 (10 contracts times 100 shares per contract times $3.30) plus a $50 commission, for a total outlay of $3,350. Although your commission would be much higher, your actual cost to enter the position would be almost $150 lower. What if the broker could also generate a $150 savings when you exited the position? Of course, by placing your own limit orders instead of market orders with an online discount broker, you may be able to achieve the same good fill at a lesser commission—you just need to know that is something you can and should do.

In addition to cheaper commissions, online discount brokers frequently also offer great ease in placing orders. The online broker I use, for example, has a tab to check if I want to open a collar. When the window opens, I just need to fill in the boxes to identify the stock I am buying, the put I am buying, and the call I am selling. In a side window, it automatically calculates the bid and ask for the combined positions. I then fill in the debit limit I am willing to pay to enter all legs simultaneously and send the order off with a single mouse click. When my order is filled, I pay a single reduced commission. My "full-service" broker offers much less convenience. In order to create a collar online with the full-service broker, I must fill out three separate orders, and I must make sure that I do not place the order to sell the calls before I place the order to buy the stock since that would place me in a naked call position. Even though I am a Level 5 trader, the online site will not permit a naked call order; I am required to call the broker to place that order if it is not done in proper sequence. As a practical matter, if I wanted to place the collar online, I would first place an order to buy the stock, then place another order to buy the puts, check to be sure the order to buy the stock is filled, and, finally, place an order to sell the calls. A full separate commission would be charged for each of the three orders. Each order would require me to go through three separate screens including my password. The alternative is to call the broker, hope he is available, and give him the order. The online discount broker makes the whole process so much easier, less time consuming, and less frustrating.

As with many things in life, a good reference can be invaluable both in the quality of the person to whom you are referred and in the time saved in finding the right individual. If you know a successful investor or trader who has a broker he likes, find out who it is. Ask what he likes about the broker and what the broker does for him. Find out whether the broker is willing to take on new clients and in what areas she specializes. Make contact and determine whether that person is willing and able to meet your trading requirements.

Types of Orders

Before choosing any broker, full-service or online discount, I suggest you determine what orders the firm makes available to its customers. For my own active trading account, I require the availability of stop loss, stop limit, trailing stop (based on either a percentage or point movement—my choice), contingent stop, one-triggers-other, and one-cancels-other orders.

These orders permit me to accomplish my objectives even when I am not actively watching the market.

Stop Loss   The stop loss order is one that tells the broker to act if, for example, a stock hits a certain price. If we bought XYZ at $34.80 as it bounced up off support at $34.50, we probably would not want to continue to hold the stock if it turned down and broke much below support. We could set a stop loss order, for example, at $34.30, which means that if the stock price dipped to $34.30, our stock would automatically be sold at the market. In other words, hitting $34.30, our stop, would immediately activate a sell order. It is important to realize that hitting the stop loss does not mean we will necessarily get the $34.30; we could get more or less.

As far as I know, no broker charges a commission for moving a stop loss order unless the order is actually filled. Therefore, you can move your stop as often as you please to protect more and more profit as a move goes in your direction without paying commission after commission. If, by chance, your broker does charge for moving a stop loss order, the answer is clear—fire him and get another broker right away.

Stop Limit   The stop limit order is essentially two orders in one. The stop portion initiates the action, and the limit sets a level that must be met or the order will not be filled. I do not use stop limits when I own or am long a position since it may not achieve my intentions. If I bought 1,000 shares of XYZ at $25, for example, and wanted to exit if the stock fell below $24, I could place a stop loss order at $24. As I described earlier, that means if the stock drops to $24 or below, my order to sell will immediately be sent to the floor as a market order. By the time my order is filled, the stock may have dropped to $23 so I would wind up getting filled at $23, but I would be out of a position that is rapidly moving against me. Better to be out at $23 than to be hanging on as it goes to $22, $21, and so on. Under the same circumstances, I could have placed a stop limit order with the stop at the same place (i.e., $24) and a limit of $23.25. When the stop is hit at $24, my sell order would now go to the market as a limit order instead of as a market order. Now I would have an order to sell at $23.25 or better. The bad news is that the stock is already at $23 and still falling so my limit could not be met; I could not get $23.25 or higher. I would still own this dog and the price would still be falling. In this case, the stop limit would actually prevent me from accomplishing my goal—getting out.

You now may be wondering why anyone should ever consider using a stop limit order. I do use them at times to buy a stock. Let us say XYZ has bumped up against a resistance at $30 several times but has never been able to break up through that level. I like the stock if it can break resistance and hit $30.50, but if it happens to move very quickly, I would not want to pay more than $32.50. In that situation, I could enter a buy stop limit order where the stop might be placed at $30.50 and the limit at $31.50. Now, if XYZ breaks through the resistance and hits my stop at $30.50, my buy order goes to the market with a limit of $31.50. If the stock price is $30.75 when my order hits the market, I will probably be filled at that number which is well within my limit. On the other hand, with the same stop limit in place, let us assume that the stock suddenly gapped up to $40. In that case, the stop portion of my order would be hit and I would have a limit order to buy at $31.50 or better. However, my limit was passed, so I would not be able to get filled at $31.50 or under. I had previously made the decision that I did not want to enter XYZ at a price greater than $31.50. Now I have the opportunity to reassess.

When buying, I definitely prefer the stop limit order to a simple buy stop. In the previous example, instead of placing a buy stop limit order, suppose I simply had placed a buy stop order at $30.50. Suddenly, some great news came out and the stock gapped up to $60. My buy stop would have been hit once the price passed $30.50 and my order would have been sent as a "buy at the market." I would own the stock, but not for the $30.50 I had been thinking, but rather for almost double that amount—$60 a share! Suppose then that the great news turned out to be a mistaken interpretation of something a company official had said. Once the news was corrected, the stock would probably dive back to its original $30 level or even below. Now I would have a loss in the area of $30 a share or so in a very short time because I had placed no limit on the price I was willing to pay for the stock. A highly unlikely scenario, you might say. Maybe so, but it has happened. Why take the chance? I simply do not buy with market orders.

Trailing Stop   Trailing stops can be absolutely fantastic. My wife and I travel a lot, and many times we may be out of touch for several days. Much as I like to trade, I am not going to take a solar-powered satellite-connected computer on a two-day float trip down a remote Alaskan river. Cruises, for example, may not be able to provide Internet connections while at sea. On those occasions when I am going to be out of pocket, I probably just do not want to close out my portfolio or simply leave stops in place. If a bullish position jumps while I am gone, I would like to be able to capture most of that jump, if possible, before it settles back to some previous level.

One type of order that satisfies my needs in these circumstances is the trailing stop loss order. When placed, the trailing stop follows the position at a predetermined percentage or amount. I usually choose a percentage when I set a trailing stop and I ordinarily place the order after the position has achieved an unrealized gain. I normally place these orders as good until canceled. Perhaps the easiest way to understand how the trailing stop works is to give an example. If I were bullish and bought ABC at $38 a share, I might wait until the stock hit $40 and then place my trailing stop. For this example, let us assume I set my trailing percentage at 2 percent. Initially, that means that if the share price fell 2 percent from $40, a drop of $0.80 to $39.20, my stop would be hit and my stock immediately sold on a market order. Since $40 a share is as high as ABC has gone since I placed my 2 percent trailing stop, $39.20 would remain the "magic number" for execution. However, if the stock price rises, so, too, does the exit. Suppose the next trade was at $40.50. In that case, a 2 percent drop from $40.50 would equal $0.81, and the $40.50 share price less the $0.81 would now move the stop up to $39.69. As you can see, as the stock price moves higher, the stop automatically moves up behind it. Once it reaches a level, it is never reduced. If the stock goes on up to $45, the stop is now 2 percent (or $0.90) lower than the new high. Now the stop would be set at $44.10 unless and until the stock price rose beyond $45. As long as the stock did not drop to $44.10 or below, the stop would not be hit.

Using a trailing point amount works essentially the same way, except that you would choose a trailing dollar or cent amount instead of a percentage. The amount chosen would then constantly set the stop point behind each succeeding new high after entry. Suppose we own a stock that is trading at $40 a share and we decide to set a $1 trailing stop. Initially, we would be stopped out if the stock dipped to $39 or below, but if the share price rose to $41, our stop would then automatically move to $40, where it would remain unless hit or unless the price moved higher, in which case the stop would also move higher. Note that as long as the trailing order is in place when we are in a bullish position, the stop will never go lower, but may continue to go higher, thus protecting more and more profit as the movement continues in the desired direction.

Trailing stops can also be used with bearish positions. If I sold XYZ short at $40, for example, I would naturally want the stock price to go down so that I could ultimately buy to cover my position at a lower price and keep the difference between the selling price and the price at which I covered. In that case, I could set a trailing stop to buy to cover if the stock price rises a percentage or dollar amount I selected. If the price is rising and I am short the stock, I am losing money, so I would place the trailing stop to close the position if the stock went up a certain percentage or dollar amount from its price at the time I set the trailing stop and from each successive new low.

Whether I am in a bullish position or a bearish position, I have found the trailing stop to be one of the most useful orders available.

Contingent Orders I have found that contingent stops also can be very helpful. A contingent stop is just what it sounds like. When a predetermined contingency is met, the stop is activated and the order sent to market. I like to use the contingent order when I am trading options and make the option order contingent on the price of the stock. For example, assume I sold the near month $35 naked put on XYZ when the stock was trading at $35.75. There is strong support at $35.30 and I do not want the stock put to me; I only sold the puts to bring in some income. I realize that there is little, if any, danger of being assigned the stock as long as the share price remains above $35, but if the price breaks below support at $35.30, who knows how low it may go. If the share price breaks below the support, I want to close my naked position ASAP. In these circumstances, I might enter a contingent order in which I say: contingent on XYZ (the stock price) going below $35.20 ($0.10 below support) buy to close the $35 puts I am short. This order would be good 'til canceled. Now, no matter where I am or what I may be doing, I know my position will automatically be closed if the stock price touches $35.20 or below. Depending on how long I have been in the position, I may have made a little or I may have a loss, but I will be out of the position and have removed the risk of being put the stock.

OTO (One-Triggers-Other) Orders   Some of the customer-oriented brokers offer additional abilities in placing orders that can be quite helpful. Interestingly, these sophisticated orders may be available at reasonably priced online brokers but may not be available through the more expensive so-called full-service brokers. One type of order that can be quite helpful is the OTO or "one-triggers-other" order. With an OTO, the trader is able to place a first order and a second order that is contingent upon the fill of the first. One use of the OTO might be when an investor owns a stock and has written (sold) a covered call. The major risk in those combined positions would arise if the stock price fell. In that event, the investor would probably be well off to sell the stock before greater losses were incurred. Of course, if the stock were sold and nothing was done about the calls that had been sold, the investor would still not only be short the calls, but also would be naked in that call position. As you know by now, selling a naked call entails very high risk (and requires a Level 5 trader), so the investor would probably want to close the short call position at the same time she sold the stock. One easy way to accomplish both those trades in a single act would be to place an OTO order. The investor could place a stop loss order (or even a trailing stop) on the stock as the first order which, if executed, would trigger another order to buy to close the call position.

Another use of an OTO would arise when the trader wanted to buy a stock or option and, when filled, immediately have a stop in place. In that situation, the first order would be to buy the stock or option, and, when that order was filled, it would trigger the second order, which would be the entry of the stop. In the best situations, the broker even enables the trader to make the stop a trailing stop.

OCO (One-Cancels-Other) Orders   For traders who may want two orders in place at the same time but want to cancel the remaining order once one is filled, the OCO (one-cancels-other) order will fill the bill. Suppose the trader buys a stock or an option and has both an upside target and a downside exit. He can place a sell to close limit order on the upside and a stop loss order at the downside exit, OCO. Now, if either side of the order is filled, the other is automatically canceled.

As you undoubtedly can see, these various orders can give us both versatility and freedom. If I have been watching a stock waiting for a break above resistance to enter a bullish position, I can place an order to buy, contingent on the stock's breaking above a certain price, with a limit on how much I will pay and that could then automatically be followed by a trailing stop if my buy order is filled. Now I can go fishing or golfing or hiking or whatever with nothing to do since my orders are all in place and require no further monitoring. I am able to set up a position where I can cut my losses and let my profits run before I ever enter.

Commissions

No discussion of brokers can be complete without addressing the subject of commissions. Every investor should be aware of the effect commissions will have on each trade. Additionally, the trader should learn what services the broker provides in exchange for those commissions.

Full-Service Brokers   As I mentioned before, you can expect to pay a higher commission with a full-service broker than you might with a deep discount online broker. The full-service broker is more likely to be more expensive for a number of reasons. They normally offer personal advice and are willing to help you with your trades. They can assist in setting goals and diversifying a portfolio. In short, there is someone to hold your hand.

The full-service firm also usually has a fairly large research and analysis staff that will provide recommendations. Each of these services may or may not be helpful. We always need to remember that advice can be bad as well as good. Though the situation has improved, I remember the day when the full-service broker would call, tout a particular stock to buy, and never call again until he was peddling another issue. Never, it seemed, would there be a call recommending a loss be cut or a stock be sold to take a profit. In fact, the story goes, as the market was crashing in 1987 and retail customers wanted to exit positions, a number of brokers simply refused to answer their telephones.

In recent years, there have been scandals relating to a few analysts recommending stock of companies with whom they maintained a relationship just to preserve that relationship. As with any profession, there are the good, the mediocre, and the bad. It is the individual investor's job to find the best and only after the broker has demonstrated ability and desire should the investor establish an account. Undoubtedly, a good full-service broker is worth high commissions. A mediocre or bad broker is worth nothing. In Chapter 3, we discussed interviewing prospective brokers. If they are disinterested in the beginning, imagine what they will be like after you entrust your portfolio to them. If they are unwilling to answer your direct questions directly, move on to the next candidate. You want to get reasonable value for the commissions you will be paying.

Find out the commission scale before you open an account. If the firm is charging $200 for an option trade, believe me, you will have a very hard—if not impossible—time making any money unless you are trading prohibitively large numbers of contracts. Unless you have more money than good sense, you probably do not want to start out by trading large numbers of option contracts.

Some of the well-known full-service brokerages began offering customers unlimited trades without commissions and charged an annual fee (paid in quarterly installments) based on the value of assets in the account. These asset-based fees in lieu of commissions generally tend to run from 1 to 1.75 percent annually and are often subject to negotiation. If one executes a large number of trades a year, the fee basis could be a pretty good deal for the trader. However, the firms instituted the asset-based fee as a benefit to themselves, not to their customers. Most investors execute very few trades a year and the asset-based fee would cost them more than the commissions on individual trades. Since active traders have taken advantage of the asset-based fee instead of paying commissions, some of the firms have now removed the "unlimited" on the number of trades and charge commissions after a predetermined number of trades have been made. As with most areas of investment, the individual needs to determine what works best for the style and number of trades he is making.

Online Discount Brokers   Once an investor has acquired sufficient knowledge and trading discipline, I favor the online broker. Generally, these firms offer reasonable commissions (under $15) to trade up to 1,000 shares of stock in most cases and $15 or under to trade up to 10 option contracts. Often, they provide the ability to place many orders quite easily, in contrast to the difficulties placing the same orders with the full-service brokers. If you want to test what I am saying, just ask a full-service broker whether they or their web site will place a contingent buy, a percentage trailing stop, an OTO, or an OCO. My bet is that the answer will be "no."

The better online brokers offer many, if not all, of those orders, and commissions are charged only when the order is executed. In addition, for the lower commission price, many provide fundamental information as well as free charts and some great educational sections. What the online discount broker usually lacks is someone to hold your hand. The commissions just do not justify the cost of keeping hand-holders on the payroll. There is someone to whom you can speak if you have difficulty placing an order or a specific question, but do not expect recommendations from a personal broker or lengthy explanations.

If you are using a deep discount broker with the very lowest commissions, make sure you know exactly what you are doing and expect only minimal service. They need to make a living and have little ability to offer help. Their job is to take your order and try to fill it—period.

The Power of Computers and the Internet

Computers and the Internet have absolutely revolutionized trading. I suppose you could still trade without a computer and the Internet, but why would you even consider it? While the theories and strategies of trading remain much the same as they have been for many years, the methods and speed have forever changed. Computers and the Internet have given the individual retail trader abilities far beyond those enjoyed 10 or even 5 years ago. Fundamental research can be done at home and without reliance on the judgment of someone who may have an unfavorable bias. Quotes for both stocks and options can be obtained in real time and orders executed within seconds. Real-time charts are also available that can supply tick-by-tick information if desired. The ambitious and motivated individual now is armed completely with whatever fundamental and technical information may be necessary to arrive at a trading decision. The logical world of facts is at hand; now the trader is left to sort through those facts and exercise the discipline required to deal with the psychological aspects of trading.

Web Sites   It is probably a valid assumption that most traders and investors will now use the Internet at least as an aid to their decision making, if not to actively make their trades. There is an absolute plethora of web sites designed to provide information to the investor. Some are available free of charge if you are willing to put up with the advertisements, and others are accessed by subscription. The ones I suspect most traders are most likely to use regularly are the brokerage web sites. If you have an account (and some brokers do not even require that it be funded), your broker's site can permit you to access a vast amount of information.

The web site for the Internet broker I use, for example, has tabs for my account, trading, quotes, a toolbox, and education. I am able to look at my account and see at a glance not only my holdings but also the daily profit and loss, cost basis, delta of my positions, and news relating to my holdings, and can immediately access a price and/or volatility chart. The "Trade" tab is further divided into windows that will take me to forms to trade stock, options, spreads, covered calls, mutual funds, bonds, and even futures. In addition, I can also go directly to a window that displays the current status of all my orders. Real-time quotes are available on a stock-by-stock (or option-by-option) basis or in a streaming matrix if I want. Information on earnings, dividend, and split dates is also available at my fingertips. I can access charts and append various indicators to them, in addition to price and volume. I can draw price supports or resistances as well as trend supports and resistances and view the charts in the form of line, bar, or candlestick.

In the "Toolbox" I have a wide variety of scans available to me when searching for specific candidates such as covered calls or naked puts. Depending on my evaluation of a specific issue, from very bullish to very bearish, the site will scan for specific strategies that meet my time parameters, money I intend to put at risk, and fit my personal trading level. My broker even offers virtual trading, which is the electronic version of paper trading so I can practice strategies without risking real money until I have developed confidence in my ability to successfully trade the strategy.

In the educational area, various windows identify and explain most, if not all, strategies utilized by traders. The explanation includes risk graphs and illustrations of profit and loss depending on stock movement. In addition, the broker conducts comprehensive web classes and holds live seminars from time to time.

The array of actions that can be taken and information available from this single firm is simply mind boggling to someone like me, who once thought the calculator was the height of electronic sophistication. Check out several of the Internet brokers and see what they offer. Explore their sites in detail before determining which firm to select.

Other sites provide information such as stock analysis, charting, upcoming items that may influence market movement, news relating to the market, individual company information, and on and on. The sheer number of financial sites is intimidating. Keep in mind that they are in business to make money, so they are either filled with advertising or trying to get you to subscribe. There is nothing wrong with either approach as long as you are aware of what is going on and make your decisions with care. As life teaches, you usually get what you pay for, so understand that the free sites may leave something to be desired. However, you might be disappointed with the content of some subscription sites, yet thrilled with what you get on others. My only advice is to check them out. Many subscription sites have a free trial period. There is nothing wrong with taking advantage of the free trial; you will see what is really offered, and the web site publisher will have the chance to show you what they have. Keep in mind that it will probably be your obligation to cancel the subscription before the end of the trial or you may be obligated to pay for some extended period.

One area of Internet subscriptions that deserves mention is the advisory service. I have been the editor of three advisory services over the past several years, and I believe they can be quite valuable to the subscriber as well as lucrative to the editor or publisher. However, all advisory services need to be approached with common sense. None, not one, is the holy grail of trading. No matter what claims are made, no advisory service provides all winners all the time. As in any trading, there will be losses as well as gains, so it is important to be aware that no service will be perfect. Even more importantly, no subscriber should substitute the information from the service for his own studied judgment. If you are going to subscribe to an advisory service, I urge you to avoid following the trade alerts blindly. Each "alert" should be nothing more than a starting point in your own decision-making process. Even though the publisher or editor probably wants you to do well so they can retain your subscription, they undoubtedly have a different business plan from yours. Their goals may differ, their risk tolerance may be markedly different, they may not be making the actual trade themselves, they may be taking larger or smaller positions than you, they may manage money in a different fashion than you, and they almost certainly have a different amount of money with which they are trading. Some who are in the business of operating advisory services do not even trade themselves; they make their income from subscriptions, not from trading. If they are unwilling to risk their own money, why should you risk yours without investigating further yourself?

Your investigation may be as simple as seeing whether the company is profitable, what its debt structure may be, and where it sits on a price chart, but you owe yourself at least that much. Failure to take steps to educate yourself about a trade before entry and establish your exit strategy is the equivalent of financial Russian roulette. My advice is to use a subscription advisory only as a starting point to narrow the list of potential candidates. If you contemplate using such a service as your complete method of trading, find some other way to make money and leave trading alone.

Speed and Memory   Since I brought up the subject of computers, I should probably address speed of operation and memory capacity. In both cases, the answer is: It depends. Generally, a great deal of memory is not critical if you are using your computer just to trade or if you have a computer solely devoted to trading. It is not like photography where you are saving images that require vast amounts of space. Even if you are keeping detailed records and journals on your trades, you are not likely to utilize a great deal of memory. Large memory usually becomes an issue only if you are using the computer for a variety of other tasks, such as manipulating photographs on Photoshop.

I prefer to dedicate a computer to my trading business and use it for no other purpose. If that is something you are able to do, I suggest you take that approach. It is then a tool devoted specifically and exclusively to your trading or investing business. No one else will have any reason to mess with it and expose it to unwanted viruses from things like extraneous e-mails. There may also be some tax advantages to using a dedicated computer in your business—check with your tax professional before you buy.

Speed brings up a slightly different issue. If you are only going to make your trading decisions over the weekend or at night and will place orders and let your account run on autopilot, you have no particular need for speed. A landline connection and a modest-speed computer is all you need. However, if you are watching the market regularly during the day and making real-time trading decisions as I often do, then you want a fairly fast processor and a high-speed connection. When I began trading for a living several years ago, no high-speed connection was available where I lived and I relied on 15-minute-delayed quotes and slow downloads. Fairly fast satellite connections became available and I signed on quickly. The speed improved dramatically, but I occasionally had problems with weather disturbances, and when I needed help, I often wound up holding on the phone for 45 minutes or more until I could speak with someone whose accent I could not understand in any event. Finally, civilization arrived in my area of rural America and I was able to have a DSL (digital subscriber line) hookup with a local provider who is extremely helpful and responsive when I encounter the rare problem. The DSL works wonderfully for me, and if you are going to be looking at real-time quotes and real-time charts, I suggest that it is an excellent choice.

Security   I cannot say this any more strongly: *Nothing* is more important about your trading computer than security. Memory, processor speed, and connection speed all take a far back seat to the need for security. In all likelihood, you will use your computer to trade, and, if you do, you will be accessing your account(s). One of the last things in the world you want is for a hacker to gain access to your assets. While I have made many suggestions in this book, I now urge and recommend that you take every precaution available to protect your trading computer. I mean you need firewalls and spyware and virus protection. This is not an option; it is an absolute, unadulterated, unmitigated necessity. Hackers are not cute when it comes to your account—they are dangerous and they are smart. Do everything you can to protect yourself against them.

There is no point in my suggesting any specific protective software, because something better will be available by the time you equip your computer. What I do urge is that you find a pro who is in the business of protecting computers for the business community and hire him to help you set up your computer protection. Pay what it costs. The peace of mind and relative safety will more than justify the cost. One web site that provides a great deal of helpful information concerning computer security is Carnegie Mellon's CERT at www.cert.org/homeusers/HomeComputer Security/.

When you assign passwords, do not use things like your husband's name or your birthday. Use something highly unlikely or even some gobbledygook with numbers and capital letters and lowercase letters mixed together. Far too many folks make it easy for hackers to guess passwords based on all too likely choices. Of course, do not leave your password lying around where others can see it and do not share it. Obviously, memorize it. If you are like me and cannot remember what you had for breakfast, keep your password in a secure place and pray you remember where you put it.

PC versus Mac   The world of computers is populated primarily with PCs and Apple computers. The PC has been by far the most popular overall and almost all financial software has been geared to it. Some financial software simply has not been compatible with the Macintosh operating systems.

Probably as a result of the PC's popularity, hackers have devoted much of their efforts to breaching PC security. I personally had a series of incidents in which a Trojan horse seeking financial information was detected by my spyware detection software. When the first breach was detected, I removed the traces of the Trojan horse with the spyware only to have the same thing reappear the following day. I then took the computer to a very competent guru and he cleaned the drive and memories for me. Again, the following day, the same culprit returned. Once again, I had the computer cleaned and then added additional security well beyond what had initially been installed. The experts concluded that it was likely that I had been specifically targeted, so I set up my accounts differently with different user names and passwords for each as well as adding the security to my computer. I learned that the PC is definitely subject to invasion by Trojan horses and viruses and must be as well armed as possible.

According to their advertisements, at least, the Mac has fewer security issues than the PC. I have been told that even if a hacker gets into the Mac, a password is required to get back out. Since I make no claim to computer expertise, I urge you to contact a true computer expert to learn the relative strengths and weaknesses regarding the security of the PC versus the Mac. The issue could be critically important.

One reason that the Mac has failed to gain the popularity of the PC with traders is that much of the financial software would only run on the PC. Even now, the charting service I use cannot be run on the Mac operating system. I understand, however, that there are now programs available for the Mac that permit the operation of PC software by creating a parallel PC on the Mac system. The parallel software then operates independently as a virtual PC on the Mac operating system. PC software then may be used on a Mac even though incompatible with the Mac's operating system.

EXPLORING AND EXPLOITING CHARTS AND CHARTING SERVICES

Fundamental analysis can tell us *what* to buy, but gives us little if any information on *when* to buy it. Technical analysis, on the other hand, can tell us when to buy and when to sell. When I write about technical analysis (or technicals) I simply mean using price and volume charts and, perhaps other indicators to assess a potential trading situation. Whether we believe history is likely to repeat itself or not, technical analysis can provide a method to trade with discipline and without emotion. Though an in-depth treatment of technical trading is beyond the scope of this book, I believe that it is critical for the investor or trader to have a grasp of at least the basic technical principles and should put that knowledge to practice in finding entries and setting exits for all trades. Unless the trader uses technicals in determining entries and exits, he is left to pure guesswork and emotion, which, to my mind, will lead to failure much more often than to success.

In order to employ technical concepts in trading, the trader absolutely must have access to charts that provide information on price and volume at the very least. These simple charts are available free of charge from many sources and can be found through a web search. As I mentioned earlier, most brokers' sites now include charts with various levels of sophistication, from those limited to price and volume to those that include the ability to overlay price support and resistance lines as well as trend lines. Some also provide additional indicators such as moving average convergence divergence (MACD), Average Directional Index (ADX), and stochastics.

The serious trader or investor can also use even more sophisticated subscription charting services. I subscribe to the same charting service that has permitted me to use their charts in this book because of the myriad of great features it provides. I can easily switch from line charts to candles and view real-time charts in any time frame from tick by tick to yearly candles or bars. I can create innumerable watchlists to include anything from my own portfolio to a set of ETFs or closed-end funds. I have the ability to create personal criteria and incorporate those criteria into scans I construct to perform rapid searches. I can sort the watchlists by a large number of categories such as price percent change today or over the last 5 days or 30 days or year; I can sort by earnings or dividends, or even categories such as percentage of shares held by institutions. I am able to overlay automatically calculated moving averages, envelopes, and Bollinger Bands over the price chart, and I can make notes directly on the charts on in a separate window if I choose. I can join or organize a group and exchange watchlists with them. The program permits me to create as many different chart templates as I want, and I am able to include various indicators such as regressions, MACD, stochastics, ADX, and even some that are proprietary to the software publisher. The program enables me to compare several charts and/or indices at the same time.

In short, the charting service is extraordinarily powerful and is an immensely useful and, once learned, easy to use tool. A subscription can cost from about $300 to under $1,000 a year depending on the features selected, and I find it hard to believe how any serious investor would want to trade without the benefits this service or others like it provide. I am sure that some will raise eyebrows over the cost and try to get by with less, but a good charting service along with the computer are the essential tools of the business. I am a believer in using the best tools available and do not think that is an area where one should skimp. If you use the best, you will find that the time and effort saved will more than make up for the cost.

Figures 9.1 through 9.3 show examples of a very small portion of the types of charts and indicators that are available. Figure 9.1 is a simple line chart depicting daily price movement over time in the upper window. The lower window shows the daily volume.

In Figure 9.2, the upper window shows daily price movement in the form of Japanese candlesticks, which show the open, close, high, and low of each day. The open candles indicate a day in which the price moved up from open to close and the filled-in candles indicate a day in which price closed lower than it opened. The middle window depicts volume, and the lower window depicts relative strength compared to the Nasdaq.

In Figure 9.3 the price is shown as a bar chart, and a 30-day moving average is overlaid in the upper window. The middle window depicts volume, and the lower window shows an indicator known as ADX.

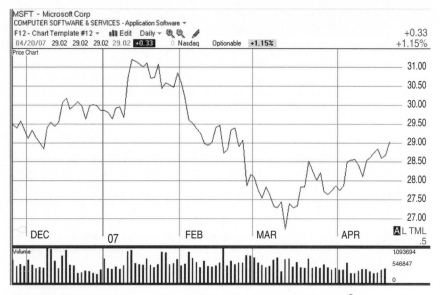

FIGURE 9.1   Line Chart with Price and Volume. (Telechart 2005® chart courtesy of Worden Brothers, Inc.)

FIGURE 9.2   Japanese Candlesticks with Volume and Relative Strength. (Telechart 2005® chart courtesy of Worden Brothers, Inc.)

FIGURE 9.3   Bar Chart with Moving Average, Volume, and ADX. (Telechart 2005®
chart courtesy of Worden Brothers, Inc.)

FURTHERING YOUR EDUCATION

While I am on the subject of cost, I also want to address the critical area
of financial education. Though society in the United States places great
emphasis on earning and accumulating wealth, it is the rare person who
has ever taken a class or attended a school where the focus was on making money. The tide may be changing in that regard, as some schools
are actually adding curriculum that does teach something about making
money, but the educational system has not yet truly embraced the concept. The general teaching community is hardly equipped to teach students
how to make or accumulate wealth. Instead, the focus largely has been on
gaining employment and performing tasks for someone else for a salary
or at an hourly rate. I remain a strong believer in the three Rs (reading,
writing, and arithmetic, for those who are not old enough to remember),
and continue to think that they are a necessary foundation to intelligent
function. Once that foundation is set, I believe it is our individual obligation and a necessity for the successful continuation of our society to
move beyond and apply those concepts to our personal quest for financial
security.

Financial education comes at a cost—a cost in time and effort that is beyond the monetary cost. However, the monetary cost is relatively small in comparison to the returns a little financial education can reap. Many of us willingly pay high taxes to further engorge the administratively top-heavy public school system, and some pay extraordinarily high private school tuitions (like $15,000 or more for kindergarten) to avoid those same public schools. Students or their parents pay more than $50,000 a semester to attend some of the best institutions of higher learning.

Since there are very few classes on learning to make money, the comparative dollar cost is small, though the effort may be great. A fairly complete trading education can probably be had for under a couple of thousand dollars. In order to get that education, you must buy and study books on investing and trading; you should buy and review DVDs or videos on trading. It takes work, time, discipline, and motivation, but the rewards are inestimable. You could spend more, perhaps on the order of $20,000 to $50,000 to attend all the best seminars and perhaps hasten the acquisition of knowledge and, again, the potential rewards could be astonishing. Compare that to the average cost per semester of college and it looks pretty good. The problem as I see it is that most people may be willing to pay for the formal traditional education that fails to teach how to make money and accumulate wealth, but refuse to spend (either in cash or effort) what it takes to learn how to really make money. If wealth creation and security is important to you, there is no easy path; you must do what it takes to gain the knowledge.

The foregoing may be a sermon to the choir since you have already taken the time and made the effort to read this far. You clearly have the desire and motivation to increase your investing knowledge. I commend you for your efforts and urge you to continue. When I began to trade, I had little money, and failure was not an option. I read everything related to trading that I could get my hands on; I attended every seminar I could afford; I watched every video and DVD I could. In other words, I paid my dues. I paper traded as I discovered new strategies and I lost and I won. I spoke to every successful trader who would give me the time. It was hard work. I still study everything I can and I set aside time each day to continue my education. I have done what others don't and now I can do what most can't in terms of my lifestyle. Has it been worth it? For me, it is more than worth it. The financial rewards have been beyond my greatest expectations. I can spend as much time with my family as I choose. I can give to my favorite charities. I can travel when and where I want and I can do almost anything I choose. Trading has given me a wonderful life, but it came at the expense of time and effort. It may or may not be for you, but, without education, it will not work.

Once the basic trading vocabulary is learned, and you probably have most of that by now, the rest is not very difficult. Study and persistent practice will take you a long way toward achieving your goals. As with any other learning, make sure you understand the basics first and build upon them. There is no need to rush, and you do not have to learn every strategy known to man. My advice is to learn three strategies that you like and that meet your risk tolerance: one for when the market is going up, one for when the market is going down, and one for when the market is going sideways. At first, what else do you need? As time goes on, learn countermeasures or fixes for plays that go against you. You may be amazed to find that there are times when something that turns against you can be turned into something very profitable.

MAINTAINING DISCIPLINE

The trader or investor has no greater enemy than emotion. Perhaps the greatest goal for trading the markets is to trade with discipline and without emotion. Contrary to popular belief, the markets operate more on the psychological than the logical. Failure is often tied to greed and to fear. It is amazing to realize how many retail investors buy at the top and sell at the bottom.

How do emotions affect our trading? Think of your own first reactions and those of your family and friends when there is a discussion of investments. "Options—oh, they're too risky." Fear. "If I'd bought 1,000 shares of Microsoft when it first went public, I'd be a multimillionaire today." Greed. "I can't sell the stock I got from my company; I might get fired if I do." Fear. "Trading is too complicated for me; I leave that to my broker." Fear. "I can triple my money when XYZ announces its earnings next week." Greed.

Why is it that many retail investors buy stock near the top and sell it near the bottom? I believe the answers are greed and fear. As a stock rises, a buzz begins. For example, several of my friends are police officers and ultimately became investors in Taser International (TASR), which markets the Taser gun, a device used in controlling unruly suspects. When information first became available about the Taser gun, some officers bought the stock. Gradually, the stock began to rise in price and they bragged about their good investment. Some more officers bought, but most still held back for fear that it might not turn out to be such a good investment. News was spread that more and more police departments were adding Tasers to their equipment and the price began to rise. The buzz got louder and was heard beyond the police community. More and more people bought the stock and bragged about their profits to those who had not yet bought. Greed was taking over, and those who had not bought for fear it might not be a good investment were now afraid they might miss out. Buying reached a crescendo as greed took over; the stock split and rose. The price finally peaked as the latecomers could not stand it any longer and jumped on the train. Now, everyone who wanted the stock had bought, and a few negative news stories began to circulate. The stock turned down, but most held their positions, greedy to add to the profits and afraid if they got out the stock might go even higher. From January to October 2005, the stock fell from a high over $30 to a low just over $5. Many held on, rationalizing their decision and believing "it'll come back." I suspect the argument within went something like this as the stock fell from $32 to $22: "It'll come back." "If it just gets back to $25, I'll sell." On it drops and, paralyzed with that terrible feeling in the pit of the stomach, the investor holds on. He no longer checks the stock price each day hoping for an upturn. Finally, the stock nears the bottom and then, giving up all hope, the investor bails out. He has run the gamut of emotions from greed at entry to fear about exiting to rationalizing why he is holding on to ultimate capitulation. None of the decisions were ruled by discipline or logic, yet most of us have followed the same or a similar course in our trading experience.

Greed can be harmful to investors in many ways. One example I have seen more often than I would like is the way in which greed pushes money management out of the picture. I once had a very bright student whose trading was going quite well. He studied hard, paper traded faithfully, and understood the strategies he was using. When he began to trade with real money, he was instantly successful. Since he had begun with a relatively small trading account, he was managing his money by making equal dollar trades. Things went so well that he was calling me almost daily; excitedly telling me how much he had made that day. "Bill," he would say, "I made $800 today." Or "I made $1,000 today." Or "I just closed one for a $500 profit." One day the phone did not ring. I did not hear from my friend the next day or the next, so I called him. "How are you doing?" I asked. "I've quit trading," he replied. "Why?" "Well, I had five winning trades in a row and I thought I knew how the stock was behaving, so I put all my money on the next trade (a bullish position), and the stock gapped down over $8 and I lost almost everything," he told me. How sad, yet how understandable was his plight. Greed had taken over and discipline went out the window. In essence, my friend made a bet instead of a disciplined trade. Discipline would have meant another equal dollar trade that would have lost part of his money, but he would still have been well ahead and would have still been in the game. Lack of discipline led to the equivalent of betting it all on black on one spin of the roulette wheel and resulted in an emotionally and financially devastating loss.

Sometimes, we become emotionally attached to our stocks, and that can be harmful as well. I once sat with an older man whom I respect and admire and reviewed his portfolio. He was concerned because it was the year 2000 and most of his positions were falling. I cavalierly told him to sell the stocks before they fell further, and his response bowled me over. "That would be like selling old friends," he said. He meant it; he was emotionally attached to his stocks simply because he had owned them for some time and because they had been gaining value until recently. I suggested that the stock prices were falling and taking money from his pockets; that they were not really old friends if they were stealing from him so it was okay to get rid of them. I suspect he remained unconvinced, and the emotional attachment to the old friends outweighed the losses they were causing.

The moral of the stories is that discipline is key. Predetermine your exits and scrupulously adhere to your money management principles. Be aware that your emotions can have a substantial and detrimental effect on your investing. You do not have to make it all in one trade, and the one trade where you think you will make it all is probably the one that will get you. The market has an uncanny way of renewing our humility.

I urge you to increase your knowledge of the power of the psychological on the markets. I recommend Dr. Alexander Elder's *Trading for a Living* (John Wiley & Sons, 2002) as a valuable next step in your trading education. Dr. Elder is a psychiatrist who trades the market successfully and brings an important perspective to the investor in *Trading for a Living* and his other books.

USING COMMON SENSE

When I used to speak to jurors in trials involving complex legal issues, I would often suggest that they not leave their common sense at the door. I reiterate that thought for the investor: do not leave your common sense out of the equation. Recently, I received the following e-mail:

Remarkable Obituary

Today we mourn the passing of a beloved old friend, Mr. Common Sense. Mr. Sense had been with us for many years. No one knows for sure how old he was since his birth records were long ago lost in bureaucratic red tape. He will be remembered as having cultivated such value lessons as knowing when to come in out of the rain, why the early bird gets the worm, and that life isn't always fair. Common Sense lived by simple, sound financial policies (don't spend more than you earn) and reliable parenting strategies (adults, not kids, are in charge).

His health began to rapidly deteriorate when well-intentioned but overbearing regulations were set in place. Reports of a six-year-old boy charged with sexual harassment for kissing a classmate, teens suspended from school for using mouthwash after lunch, and a teacher fired for reprimanding an unruly student only worsened his condition.

Mr. Sense declined even further when schools were required to get parental consent to administer aspirin to a student but could not inform parents when a student became pregnant and wanted to have an abortion. Finally, Common Sense lost the will to live as the Ten Commandments became contraband; churches became businesses; and criminals received better treatment than their victims. Common Sense finally gave up the ghost after a woman failed to realize that a steaming cup of coffee was hot and was awarded a huge financial verdict.

Common Sense was preceded in death by his parents, Truth and Trust; his wife, Discretion; his daughter, Responsibility; and his son, Reason. He is survived by two stepbrothers: My Rights and Ima Whiner. Not many attended his funeral because so few realized he was gone.

Author Unknown

As you approach your trading, I suggest you do so using your common sense. I do not mean that you should expect the behavior of the market to be based on common sense; much of its movement will be the result of emotional reaction. If you can use common sense to predict the emotion, you have a good chance to be ahead of the crowd. Apply common sense and rationality to your entries and to your money management. Be reasonable in your expectations.

HELPFUL INDICATORS

So far in this chapter, we have addressed a number of the basic aids to successful trading. Since there are no certainties in successful investing, we seek any edge we can get. There are a couple of indicators that I have found to be helpful and are worthy of discussion.

Volatility

Basically, volatility is a measure of how fast prices are changing. For example, when a stock or a market is experiencing wide price swings in short time periods, volatility is high. On the other hand, if price movements are relatively slow and fairly flat, volatility is low. Several measures of volatility are available. Perhaps the most commonly used is the VIX, which is the CBOE Market Volatility Index. I also like to look at the VXN, which is the CBOE Nasdaq Volatility Index, and the VXO, the CBOE OEX Volatility Index. These measures are generally readily available through subscription charting services or on brokerage web sites.

Volatility can give some indication of future market direction. When volatility is moving up, markets tend to be moving down, and when volatility is moving down, markets tend to be moving up. I watch volatility for turns from extremes. As volatility ascends, I look for it to top out and turn over. As high volatility begins to turn over and start down, I begin to look for and enter bullish positions. If volatility is continuing to descend, there is some assurance that I can remain in bullish positions without bringing stops too tight. Conversely, when volatility has descended and begins giving indications that it is starting to turn back up, I watch more closely for a market downturn and consider tightening stops on my existing bullish positions.

Like anything else in trading, volatility can show false signals on occasion. It may be at a low level and give a little head fake, moving up only to dip again. I mention this to emphasize that volatility is not a perfect indicator, but neither is anything else I have found. It is an assistant only and can help obtain that little edge that makes mediocre trading good or good trading great.

Options traders should also be aware of the concept of implied volatility. Implied volatility is essentially the market's prediction of where prices are going. It is distinguished from what is known as historical or statistical volatility in that statistical volatility is an actual historical measurement of volatility such as we see with the VIX or VXN. Implied volatility is, in effect, the market's guess of future movement. Implied volatility provides the options trader with a sense of whether the options are "cheap" or "expensive." Options that are in the lower 15 percentiles of implied volatility, for example, could be considered to be relatively cheap, while those in the upper 15 percentiles could be considered expensive. Volatility traders look to buy cheap options (those in the lower percentiles of implied volatility) and sell expensive options, but that is the subject of a whole other book.

Put/Call Ratio

Another helpful indicator is the put/call ratio. It is calculated simply by dividing the volume of put contracts by the volume of call contracts. The ratio can usually be found on your broker's web site, but if it is not available there, it is published on the CBOE (Chicago Board Option Exchange) along with a great deal of other useful information. The put/call ratio is a measure of option trader sentiment. If the number is high, it is an indication that sentiment is bearish because put contracts are outnumbering call contracts. If the number is low, sentiment is bullish.

The put/call ratio is generally considered to be a contrarian indicator at the extreme ends. The theory goes that if the whole market is thinking in one direction, it is probably wrong and a turn can be expected. When the put/call ratio is very high (bearish), look for the market to turn up, and when the put/call ratio is very low (bullish), look for the market to turn down.

I try to look at the put/call ratio in conjunction with the VIX and VXN to see if I can get an indication that the market is getting ready to turn or has begun to turn.

MY TRADING CREDO

Throughout this book, I have set out a great deal of methodology and strategy. I now want to expand those elements to include some additional principles and beliefs that can heighten the likelihood of ultimate success.

Patience

When I was a kid, my mother used to tease me saying: "Patience is a virtue, possess it if you can; often found in women, but never found in men." Perhaps that is the reason why women often make better traders than men. Impatience can definitely be the enemy when trading the markets. All too often, for example, I have seen students rush to begin trading with real money rather than perfecting their use of strategies by paper trading. I have often received e-mails from advisory service subscribers inquiring about making real money trades using strategies they have never attempted before. Invariably, my advice is to learn the strategy first by paper trading, and only after the paper trading is successful should they consider using real money. Impatience is fueled by greed. Impatient exuberance about entering a trade hides the realization that it could be a loser instead of a winner. A little patience can go a long way. Knowledge must precede any trade, and knowledge can be gained only through patient study. You may have heard the saw that if you are willing to do for 6 or 12 months what others won't (i.e., study, plan, learn), you may be able to do for the rest of your life what others can't (i.e., live the quality lifestyle of your dreams). That approach demands patience as well as determination and diligence.

The need for patience manifests itself in many ways for the trader. A good trader will wait for the right entry. If the investor is interested in a specific stock that is still moving down, he knows it is not yet time to buy because who knows where or whether the descent will stop. Instead, the patient trader will await an upturn before entering the position. Trying to catch a falling piano may not be a good idea, so why not wait until the stock gives some indication that it is ready to move in the direction you want?

Inexperienced or unsuccessful traders may also be impatient to find a trade to enter. They have a tendency to make a trade just for the sake of trading rather than wait to find one that has a real chance of success.

Impatience can also be the enemy when exiting a trade. The problem often arises when the trade has become profitable on paper. All too many investors become impatient and fearful and take their profits much too early. They bail out on the slightest retracement only to watch the position take off after they have exited. The patient trader realizes that there will be retracements and trails the position with a stop or at least some exit strategy that accounts for the likelihood of occasional dips. The use of a percentage-trailing stop, for example, can remove the emotion and impatience from a trade. Good decisions are made out of the heat of battle so that both emotion and impatience are removed from the trading equation.

Resilience

Losses are an inevitable part of trading. In order to achieve ultimate success, one need only have more profit than loss. When losses do come, the investor must be resilient. She needs to manage her money so that no loss or even series of losses will take her out of the game. As I explained in the Money Management section in Chapter 3, using a method such as limiting each investment to an equal percentage of risk money (perhaps 3 to 5 percent per trade) will keep us in the game even through a series of losses. Suppose we have $100,000 in risk money and that we choose to make trades equal to 3 percent of our risk and suppose we lose all the money we put at risk for five trades in a row. In the first trade, we would lose $3,000, so now our risk money would be down to $97,000. In the second trade, we would lose $2,910, and we would be down to $94,090. We lose $2,822 in the third trade and so on until after the fifth trade we are left with around $85,875. We are still in the game and we still have plenty of cash with which to invest. Our money management plan has made us resilient financially.

We also need to be emotionally resilient. In the preceding example, I envisioned a situation where we had a total loss of our money at risk in five successive trades. While we might realistically lose five times in a row, it would be highly unlikely that we would lose everything risked in each of those trades unless we happened to be in a coma. However, if we did lose everything risked in five successive trades, we would undoubtedly have an adverse emotional reaction. Something like, "Oh, I just can't do this" or "Trading isn't for me" would probably enter our minds. However, the truth is that failure is not permanent. Yes, these trades may not have worked, but it does not mean that we are a failure. It only means that we had some losing trades. If we return to our common sense, we realize that we knew before we started that we would have some losing trades. Now we had some. Something happened that we knew from the outset would happen. We also knew we would have some winners.

There Is No Holy Grail

What are the chances that a stock price will go up tomorrow? I really do not know, but it certainly seems like it would be 50 percent. Whether it is 50 percent or not could certainly be argued because historically the market goes up more than it goes down, but when it goes up, it sometimes tends to go up in a spurt rather than steadily and then may retrace a bit. So what day is it going to spurt up and what day is it going to retrace? What makes the price of a stock move? Clearly, it could be news about the company, whether the news is good or bad. What if we could have tomorrow's newspaper and could see the news in advance. What would we do? First, I would buy a lottery ticket, but knowing the news would also give us a tremendous advantage in making investment decisions. Fundamental information about a company can also influence the price but tells us nothing about when the price will respond, and even if the fundamental news is great, will it necessarily overshadow the news of some world event? I am sure that some company or companies had fantastic news on the afternoon of September 10, 2001, but how did their stock perform the morning of 9/11 after the attack and before the markets were closed?

Since no mathematical formula could ever account for all of the variables that coalesce at any given moment to result in the price of a stock and since psychology also plays a significant part in price movement it seems impossible that any mathematical model could ever be constructed to provide a precise prediction of a market or stock price. Hence, there can be no holy grail of trading. That does not mean, however, that we should not trade; it only means that there can be no perfect trading.

I am addressing this issue as a result of certain personality traits I have encountered in some students. One fellow I know has spent at least four years trying to construct the perfect trading model. He refuses to trade until his quest is fulfilled. He has created a club or group on a subscription chart service and promises each year that his work is nearing completion. Sadly, he fails to recognize that trading perfection is beyond reach. If he could create a system that yielded positive results 70 or 80 percent of the time and combined that with good money management, he could be rich beyond his dreams, yet fear of even one loss prevents him from trading.

When we seek the holy grail of trading, we can easily succumb to paralysis of analysis. I have seen students who are terrified to make a trade because they do not believe they have gathered and analyzed every piece of technical and fundamental information. Since they cannot ever satisfy themselves that they have made an exhaustively complete analysis, they will not act. They fail to realize that it does not matter. Even if they could achieve the objective of total and complete analysis of every relevant fact, what is to say that something could not change as they click their mouse to send off an order?

The truly successful investor realizes and accepts that trading perfection is unattainable. Of course, both mathematical formulae like technical indicators and analysis can reduce the likelihood of a loss, but they cannot insure success. The closest thing to the holy grail of trading, then, is to learn to cut losses in a disciplined fashion with as little emotion as possible and to let profits run in a disciplined fashion with as little emotion as possible. It is perfectly appropriate and helpful to use both analysis and mathematical formulae to assist in those tasks in order to try to gain an edge, but it is counterproductive to expect to achieve perfection.

Do Not Be Afraid to Take Profits

Recently, one brokerage firm has spent a great deal of money on TV ads suggesting that all investing should be long term. While I concede that history has shown that markets do go up over long periods, I am concerned about the investor who buys into the proposition that all investments should be long term and then needs his money for some emergency when the markets or his equities are down. The TV ads fail to mention that the Nasdaq Composite Index was over 5,000 in early 2000 and seven years later is about half that number. Is that broker telling you that you should have sat through a drop of around 3,900 points on the index and still be holding at the bottom? I think I would prefer to have taken my profits after the index turned down and not watched the value of my portfolio drop almost 78 percent—but that's me.

Since the "Qs" (QQQQ) track the Nasdaq, it may be helpful to further explore my point by looking at them over the same time frame (early 2000 to early 2007; see Figure 9.4). QQQQ topped near 110 in January 2000. The TV ads with which I have a problem advocate holding on to a position. By late 2001, the Qs had hit an intermediate bottom around $29. Instead of holding on during the 81-point 73 percent crash, I would advocate having sold short, for example. Instead of being down 81 points, suppose I had closed my long position (which the TV ad tells you not to do) and gone

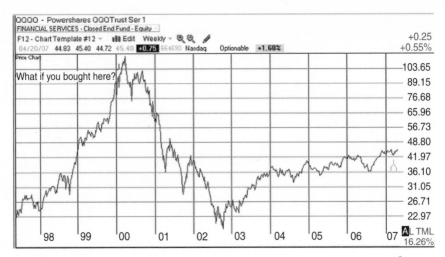

FIGURE 9.4   Weekly Chart of QQQQ from 1997 to 2007. (Telechart 2005[®] chart courtesy of Worden Brothers, Inc.)

short. Suppose I went short after QQQQ dipped below the 50-week moving average around $80 and held until a bounce off the $29 intermediate bottom. Now, instead of having sat there with my teeth in my mouth and my financial emotions in turmoil, I would have made about $50 a share on the downward move. The Qs followed with another down leg, finally taking them to the $20 area—another opportunity to play the downside and pick up another $25 or $30 a share while our TV adviser had been advising to sit tight. Which approach do you prefer? If you are willing to obtain the knowledge and then control your own portfolio, their TV advice is unadulterated nonsense. If you followed the TV ad's advice while buying QQQQ in early 2000, you would be down about $65 a share from the top seven years later. Even worse, suppose you had entered a position in the Qs at $50 a share in 1999 and it went to $110, but you followed the TV advice. You would have left a $60-a-share profit on the table and seven years later still would not be back to even. What if you had an emergency in late 2000 and had to take out your money? You get the picture. All advice is not necessarily good advice, even if you see it on a TV ad.

Another "genius move" occurs when a person has entered a position that became profitable and then watches as it turns into a monumental loss. Why did they fail to sell and take profit before the stock dropped into the unrealized loss column? "I didn't want to have to pay taxes," all too often, is the nonsensical answer. First, the taxes are paid only on the gain, not the whole position, and, second, if the position has been held the requisite time, it is a long-term capital gain and currently taxed at even lower rates than regular income. Short-term gains generally are taxed at regular income rates. So what? Pay the tax.

Suppose I am in a position where I have $10,000 in profit and I have held it more than a year. My tax will be on the $10,000 and currently would amount to 15 percent or $1,500, so, overall, I would keep $8,500 of the $10,000 gain plus, of course, my original investment. What if the stock turned down in price and the gain was reduced to $5,000. Now, after taxes, I would still keep $4,250 of the gain. Suppose, though, I continued to watch the price fall because I did not want to pay taxes and now I am in a position where I have a $2,000 loss. Am I better off for not taking the profit and paying the taxes? Of course not; I am much worse off. I once had an after-tax gain of $8,500. Now I have a loss of $2,000. Overall, my brilliant decision not to sell at a profit has cost me $10,500. What kind of logic is that? What happened to the common sense?

Be Wary of Investment Clubs and Trading Groups

I must confess that I am somewhat negative about investment clubs and trading groups. Some I concede are excellent and quite successful. Many, however, are a serious disappointment. Investment clubs are usually groups who pool some money, discuss potential trades, and use the pooled money to make the trades. Unfortunately, investment clubs often become little more than a group that argues about what stock they are going to buy, and once bought, wind up pointing fingers at one another if the trade does not go well. I am definitely not an advocate of trading by committee. Sometimes hard decisions need to be made, and most group decisions tend to be compromises, often leaving some members dissatisfied. At times, investment clubs are led by someone who exercises too much control and, at other times, someone who does too little. Just be aware of the issues that can and do arise and decide whether or not you would be better off doing your own trading.

Trading groups are a bit different in that the members do not pool money and make trades with it. Instead, they tend to be more of a social group where members may exchange trading ideas and speakers may make presentations concerning anything from strategies to software. Often, the speakers are selling something and, at times, the trading group leader may be getting a kickback on the sales. Certainly there is nothing wrong with the practice as long as the members are aware of the relative agendas. While the educational opportunities may be quite positive, they also can be confusing. The meetings tend to present the "idea of the week" or the "idea of the month," and though each idea may have real value, members can tend to jump from one to the other without completely understanding or testing the information. Again, there is the never-fulfilled search for the holy grail of trading. One additional concern is that many members of the group might be failures as traders, yet they are constantly exchanging their unsuccessful strategies and methods with one another. All that having been said, there is nothing wrong with investigating a trading group as long as you are aware of and avoid the pitfalls.

Some investment clubs and some trading groups are wonderful, successful, and informative. Those are the ones you want to find if you are interested in group interaction. I would suggest, however, that you might seek out some proven successful traders in your area and see if they would agree to let you pick their brain.

DO'S AND DON'TS

Much of this information has been mentioned before, but I've put it together as a helpful checklist of key "do's" and "don'ts" for all traders.

Don'ts

1. Don't trade more than you can afford to lose. The "bet it all on black" theory might bring a huge windfall, but, more often, it will lead to bankruptcy.

2. Don't enter any position without a predetermined exit in case the play turns against you. When someone buys a stock and it drops, the tendency seems to believe that "it'll come back." It may or it may not. Remember, though, if a stock drops 50 percent, it has to go up 100 percent just to get back to even. It is said that the first loss is the best loss. Unfortunately, the average retail trader holds on too long when a play heads in the wrong direction. Instead of using a predetermined exit, he may wait for his position to reverse back into positive territory or at least gain back some lost ground until finally abandoning it in frustration. Meanwhile, he has wasted time and the opportunity to have his money work for him.

3. Don't exit prematurely if the move is going in your direction. Just because there is a good profit does not mean that it can't go higher. Instead of selling during a good move, consider trailing a stop loss order or use the violation of a moving average or a trend line as your exit.

4. Don't be impatient.

5. Don't let emotion rule your trading. Have a business plan and stick to it. Discipline yourself to enter and exit by your own predetermined rules. Some advocate cutting losses when a position is down 5 to 8 percent; others suggest an exit on the violation of a moving average; and still others may advise exiting on the break through a price or trend support

or resistance. It is more important that you choose some method, any method, such as one of those just mentioned than have no method at all.

6. Don't enter a trade unless you fully understand and appreciate the risks.

Do's

1. Learn as much as possible about trading and trading strategies.

2. Develop a personal business plan before you make your next trade and follow your plan.

3. Have a money management plan in place and follow it. Money management is one of the most critical factors influencing your success.

4. Have an entry and an exit plan before you ever enter a position and stick to it.

5. Keep your expectations reasonable. Do not expect to win every trade. Realize that any given trade could yield 35 percent or 150 percent in a month, but that does not mean you can annualize the amount and be assured that you will make 420 percent or 1,800 percent a year. That, too, can be done, but is it a reasonable expectation?

6. Make your own educated decisions. No one will ever care as much about your money as you do. Apply your own knowledge and use your common sense; do not blindly follow others.

7. Understand a strategy before you use it and make sure you recognize exactly what is at risk in each trade.

8. Evaluate the potential reward in the trade to the risk you are taking. If you are entering a bullish position, for example, see how much you are risking by determining your exit and then see where the next resistance appears to be. The distance from entry point to first resistance is the number you should use to calculate your potential reward. That potential reward should then be divided by the potential risk to see whether you want to enter the trade. I would suggest a reward-to-risk ratio of at least 2.5:1 before entering a trade. In other words, you want the potential reward to be at least two and a half times the risk you are going to take or you should pass on the trade.

9. If you are going to pay attention to what someone else has to say about trading, make sure it is someone who is successful. Uncle Louie, the parking lot attendant who has never made a trade in his life, may not be the best person to listen to about trading.

10. Never stop learning. Put aside some time each day or at the very least each week to continue your trading education. I would be surprised if you ever run out of new information. So far, I can tell you I have not.

CONCLUSION

We have come a long way from the beginning, and all that is left for now is a comparison of the strategies to which you have been exposed in this book. It is my sincere hope that you have seen new ways to generate and increase your wealth while keeping risk contained. If I have achieved my goal, you can now face the formerly daunting world of stock and option investment with confidence and the knowledge that you can change your life for the better. Your future is in your hands. Use your newfound knowledge and confidence to go forward and establish your security for the future. You can do it; now you know you can.

CHAPTER 10

Comparison of Strategies

This chapter will summarize, review, and compare strategies we have covered throughout the book. You'll need to decide for yourself what strategies are appropriate for your own particular circumstances and inclinations. In making those decisions, you should be aware of your experience level, risk tolerance, ability to discipline your trading, amount of risk money with which you will begin, the time you are able and willing to devote to trading, and the elements of your business plan.

In comparing the strategies, each section will set out the relative amount of capital required, the expected market and stock direction, the relative level of risk undertaken, a predicted time frame, the potential reward, the preferred implied volatility (IV) for options, how closely positions need to be monitored, and what steps might be taken to provide some level of protection.

Following the narrative I will set out a synopsis for each strategy in list form for quick review.

THE COLLAR

The safest play of all is the collar, where the investor simultaneously buys the stock, buys at-the-money puts, and sells an out-of-the-money call. The premium for the calls that are sold will be large enough that it covers most or all of the cost of the puts. If the premium received for the calls pays for the puts, the worst thing that could happen would be that the stock fell in price by option expiration. In that case, the investor would simply exercise the puts, sell the stock, and wind up with no loss—a true zero-risk trade. Of course, if he were able to sell the out-of-the-money call for more than he paid for the at-the-money puts, the worst case would be that he would still make a profit even if the stock price fell.

Though quite safe, the collar strategy does have some drawbacks. Since the investor is buying stock, a fair amount of capital may be required. In recent times, I have noticed that collars have been working better for me with higher-priced equities. Also, though risk is quite limited or even absent, the reward is also capped. In my experience, I have seen the occasional collar where the upside potential may hit the 30+ percent per year range, but most fall somewhere under 20 percent. Generally speaking, we need to be in these trades for a relatively long period such as a year or so.

The protection is incorporated in the strategy for a collar. Generally speaking, we are looking for a market, sector, and stock that are mildly bullish to bullish for this strategy.

Synopsis of Collars

Relative risk: Low to zero, and even sometimes guaranteed profit at time of entry

Capital required: High

Potential reward: Limited by strike price of calls sold

Time frame: One year or more

Expected market direction: Mildly bullish to bullish

Protection: Built in

Intensity of investor monitoring: Very little

BUYING STOCK WITH PROTECTIVE PUTS

Buying stock along with protective puts is another relatively safe but capital-intensive strategy. With this strategy, the worst-case scenario is that we can assign the stock at the strike price of the put anytime before the options expire. If we buy at the money puts when we buy the stock, the most we can lose if we have to exercise the put is the price we paid for the put plus commissions, of course. The risk is greater if we buy out of the money puts, since it is then equal to the price of the put plus the difference between the price at which we bought the stock and the strike at which we can assign it.

The potential rewards of this strategy are virtually unlimited, but we must remember that the stock price must increase more than the initial cost of the puts if we hold until expiration in order to achieve a profit. In the event we decide to sell the stock before our puts expire, the puts may still have some value, so we could sell them at the same time or just convert to a straight put play by retaining the puts if we have reason to believe that the stock may be turning down.

I would prefer to buy the protective put when the IV is in the lower percentiles, though it may not be as important as when simply buying a directional option.

Anytime we are buying stock, our outlook is bullish. That is certainly the case when buying a stock along with a protective put. We want to see the stock price go up as fast as it can and at least move up before our puts expire. Naturally, this movement can occur in any time frame and is limited only by the expiration date of our puts and our willingness to roll the puts out to later expirations if we have not seen the stock move quickly enough.

Synopsis of Buying Stock and Protective Puts

Relative risk: Low and limited by the puts purchased

Capital required: High

Potential reward: Unlimited

Time frame: Limited by expiration of puts purchased

Expected market direction: Bullish

Implied volatility sought: Prefer to have lower IV but not critical

Protection: Built into strategy

Intensity of investor monitoring: Low to moderate

SELLING STOCK SHORT AND BUYING PROTECTIVE CALL

Just as buying a stock with a safety net of protective puts is a relatively low-risk and certainly controlled-risk bullish strategy, selling a stock short and buying a protective call is a controlled-risk bearish strategy. In this strategy, no capital is invested since the play begins with the sale of borrowed stock and a flow of cash into the account. The cost of the protective calls is paid from the credit received.

The time frame of a short sale and purchase of protective calls is influenced by two relatively significant factors. First, the expiration date of the calls is important since, once expired, there is no protection against an upward move except that which might be provided by stops. Second, the investor needs to be aware that he will be paying interest on the borrowed stock so the less time in the short position, the less the effect of the interest.

As long as the protective call is in place and assuming an at-the-money or out-of-the-money call, the risk is limited to the difference between the strike price of the call and the initial sale price of the stock plus the cost of the calls plus interest. In other words, if an at-the-money call is purchased, the risk during the life of the call is limited to the price of the call plus interest.

The potential reward is limited only by the price for which the stock is sold at entry. If, for example, the stock were sold at $50, the maximum gain per share could be only $50 since a stock price cannot go below zero. If the investor can sell a falling stock, profits can accumulate quite quickly with this strategy.

If we do make a relatively fast profit and there is still time left until expiration, we may be able to sell our calls and recoup some of that cost as well. In the alternative, we could hang on to the calls if it looked like the stock price were turning up and attempt to reduce the loss on the calls or even enjoy a profit on them if the stock moved far enough before expiration.

Synopsis of Selling Stock Short and Buying Protective Calls

Relative risk: Low and limited by the calls purchased

Capital required: Opened with a credit but some money on hold (check with broker)

Potential reward: Unlimited to a stock price of zero

Time frame: Limited by expiration of calls purchased and cost of interest

Expected market direction: Bearish

Protection: Built in

Intensity of investor monitoring: Moderate

CREDIT SPREADS

Credit spreads involve positions in more than one option at the same time. In the case of credit spreads, the option that is sold is more expensive than the option that is bought, so a credit comes into the account the next day. The risk is limited to the spread between the strike prices less the credit received times the number of shares.

Bullish Put Spread

When an investor expects an investment to be neutral to somewhat bullish, the bullish put credit spread provides a limited and controlled risk with a limited reward. Often, though, the limited reward provides quite a good return on risk in a relatively short time. While a credit spread can be placed using options with relatively long-term expirations, I greatly prefer to use those with a near-term expiration, many times with only a couple of weeks to go.

In the bull put spread, we are selling the higher-strike put and buying the lower strike. The initial risk is the difference between the two strikes times the number of shares. For example, if we entered a spread of 10 contracts a side, selling the April $40 puts and buying the April $35 puts, the spread would be $5 and the initial risk $5,000 ($5 times 10 contracts times 100 shares per contract). However, the market would pay us a credit to enter the positions since we would be getting more money from the sale of the $40 puts than we would pay for the $35 puts. If we got a $1 credit, we could receive $1,000 ($1 times 10 contracts times 100 shares per contract) less commissions when we entered the trade. Since we keep that $1,000, our risk would be reduced to $4,000 and our return on risk would be 25 percent (as long as the stock price stayed above $40 until expiration). The potential reward is limited to the amount of credit received when the position is opened.

Since these spreads are entered for a credit—the market is paying me to get in—no capital outlay is required. However, we need to be aware that the amount at risk is placed "on hold" in our account until expiration or until the position is closed.

Bearish Call Spread

As the name indicates, we can use a bearish call credit spread when we perceive a bearish leaning to a market, sector, or stock. As with the bullish put spread, the bearish call spread offers limited risk with limited reward. Again, though limited, the reward can provide a handsome return on risk in quite short time frames. Since a credit is obtained at entry, there is no capital outlay, though the amount at risk is "on hold" until the position is closed or the options expire.

Synopsis of Credit Spreads

Relative risk: Limited

Capital required: Opens with a credit and only amount at risk on hold

Potential reward: Limited to initial credit (unless adjusted)

Time frame: Usually short

Expected market direction: Neutral to bullish for bull put or bearish for bear call

Protection: Limited risk from long leg

Intensity of investor activity: Need fairly close monitoring

DEBIT SPREADS

Debit spreads, like credit spreads, involve positions in more than one option at the same time. A major difference is that these debit spreads are opened with an outflow of cash from the account instead of an influx of cash. The only capital required is the initial cost to enter the spread. These spreads also offer risk limited to the amount of the initial investment and also permit only a limited reward. Since these spreads are net purchases, I prefer to enter positions with longer time frames and generally choose options with expirations that are four to six months away.

Bullish Call Spread

When we have reason to expect an upward movement in our underlying, we can attempt to profit by buying a lower strike call and selling a higher strike call. Normally, we buy a call that is at-, near-, or slightly in-the-money and sell the call that is a strike price higher. The sale of the higher-strike call, while placing an upper limit on the potential reward, also reduces the cost to enter the trade and, therefore, limits the size of the risk.

If XYZ were trading at $202, for example, we might buy the four-month-out $200 call for $15.70 and sell the $210 call for $10.70. Our cost would be $5 plus commissions and we would have $5 at risk. If XYZ got to $210 by expiration, our $200/$210 spread would be worth $10. We had $5 risk to begin and would make a $5 profit, for a 100 percent gain before commission in four months. What if the stock got to only $207 by expiration? In that case, our $200 call would be $7 in-the-money and we would sell it and take in $7. In that case, we would still have a $2 profit on our $5 investment, for a 40 percent return. The $210 call would expire worthless. What if the stock went to $203 and stalled? At expiration, our $200 call would be worth $3.

We would lose $2. The only time we would lose our whole $5 investment would be if we reached expiration and the stock were below $200.

Bearish Put Spread

In the bearish put spread, the trader buys the put at- or near-the-money (or even in-the-money sometimes) and sells some strike price below that. Again, the risk is limited to the amount invested plus commission and the reward is limited by the lower strike of the put that is sold. As with the bull call spread, I like four- to six-month expiration since the play is a net purchase and I prefer to give it some time to work. Obviously, we are expecting a bearish move when we enter a bear put spread.

Suppose it looks like ABC is ready to drop. Currently, it is trading at $40.60. The five-month-out $40 put is trading at $2.30 and the $35 puts can be sold for $0.70. We could buy the $40s and sell the $35s for a net cost before commission of $1.60. If the stock drops to $35 or below by expiration, we can take in $5 and have a profit of $3.40 on our $1.60 investment. That would be a 212.5 percent return before commission. If ABC only dropped to $38 by expiration, our $40 put would be worth $2, still giving us a $0.40 profit (+25 percent).

Profitability of either of these debit spreads is dependent on a directional movement of the stock within the life of the options, but can provide some pretty spectacular returns.

Synopsis of Debit Spreads

Relative risk: Limited to initial investment

Capital required: Limited and, depending on number of contracts, can be low

Potential reward: Limited to the spread less the cost of entry

Expected market movement: Up for bull call spread; down for bear put spread

Protection: Built in and risk limited to initial investment

Intensity of investor monitoring: Moderate to high

IRON CONDOR

The iron condor is a combination of two spreads. We place a bear call spread and a bull put spread and generate income from both as we open the positions. I like to place the bear call spread so that the lower strike call (the one I am selling) is at the first strike above resistance and place the bull put spread so that the higher strike put (the one I am selling) is the first strike below support. As long as the stock price stays between the strike of the short put and the short call at expiration, we get to keep the whole credit we obtained when we opened the positions. Our upside potential is limited to the initial credits received. Since a stock can be at only one price when options expire, the worst-case scenario is that only one of the two spreads can be a loser.

In an iron condor, we are looking for the stock to trade in a range between the strike price of the put we sold and the strike price of the call we sold so the strategy is geared to relatively neutral market expectancy.

Capital requirements are generally not too great, though we must consider that we are going to pay four commissions to enter the positions and may wind up paying more if we close one or more legs of the spreads to adjust during the life of the play.

Since this strategy involves net credits to the account that are generated from the sale of time value alone, I prefer to use near-term expirations, usually no more than five or six weeks at the longest.

Synopsis of Iron Condors

Relative risk: Limited

Capital requirements: Low to moderate with a fairly heavy commission burden

Potential reward: Limited to credit received (unless adjusted)

Expected market direction: Relatively neutral

Protection: Built in by the purchase of the long calls and long puts

Intensity of investor monitoring: Moderate

BUYING CALLS

The "buying calls" strategy is as bullish as it gets. When we buy a call, we want the stock price to move higher and we want it to move higher quickly. The risk is limited to the amount we pay for the calls, which is another way of saying that 100 percent of our investment is at risk. The capital required to buy calls is usually significantly less than what would be required if we were to buy the actual stock so we normally do get quite a bit of leverage when we purchase calls.

When I search for a call-buying opportunity, I am looking for a bullish underlying and I seek calls that are both cheap (low percentile of IV) and undervalued (statistical volatility [SV] is higher than IV). Since time will be running against me whenever I buy an option, I prefer to buy a great deal of time; certainly no less than four full months. More often than not, I consider buying Long-Term Equity Anticipation Securities (LEAPS) with a year or two remaining until expiration. I also usually choose a strike with a delta near 0.70.

Buying calls is ordinarily considered to be a limited-risk, unlimited-reward strategy. While that is an accurate generalization and while the potential reward is unlimited, the unskilled trader can and frequently does increase the odds against his own possible success. One common way to cause risk to skyrocket is to buy short-term out-of-the-money calls. The unwary fall into this trap because the premiums can be very low, but for a very good reason. The chances of failure are great and the chances of success slight. If we buy out-of-the-money options, we are paying for nothing but time, and time runs against us from the moment we enter the play. Time value diminishes at a higher and higher rate the closer the option gets to expiration, so buying short amounts of time can be a particularly dangerous strategy. Another way to increase the odds of losing is to hang on to a long call position until expiration hoping the stock price will jump. In cases like that, the saying is: "Hope rhymes with dope."

Overall, we can reduce risk by buying in-the-money longer-term calls and having an exit strategy in place from the beginning. If I do not see some positive directional movement fairly quickly (like the first month or so I own LEAPS), I consider using time as my exit and move on to something else. I almost never hold a long option position past the halfway mark to expiration.

Synopsis of Buying Calls

Relative risk: Limited, but limited to the whole investment

Capital required: Low to moderate compared to buying stock

Potential reward: Unlimited

Time frame: Any, but I prefer to buy no less than four months and usually much more

Expected market direction: Very bullish

Implied volatility: Buy calls where the IV is in the low percentiles and is below SV

Protection: None—the whole investment is at risk

Intensity of investor monitoring: High; requires close monitoring

BUYING PUTS

Almost everything in the preceding section about buying calls applies to buying puts. The obvious exception is that buying puts is a bearish strategy, and when you buy puts you want the underlying to go down in price and you want to see that happen relatively quickly. Perhaps a somewhat less obvious difference is the amount of time to buy. Again, we definitely want to avoid short-term out-of-the-money plays, but I do not believe it is necessary to buy LEAPS puts. My own preference when buying puts is to buy expirations about four to six months out. It seems that when drops occur they happen fairly quickly, so there is not a need for as much time.

In a put buy, I am also willing to take a lesser delta (perhaps –0.45 or so) than when buying calls where I look for a delta near 0.70. As in the case of calls, I look for puts with a low percentile of IV and a situation where the IV is below the SV. When I find that combination, I can be reasonably certain that I am buying relatively cheap, undervalued options.

The risk is limited when buying puts, but, once again, it is limited to the whole initial investment. Reward is unlimited down to a stock price of zero.

Synopsis of Buying Puts

Relative risk: Limited, but limited to the whole amount invested

Capital requirement: Relatively low depending on strike and expiration

Potential reward: Unlimited to a stock price of zero

Time frame: Any, but I prefer four to six months

Expected market direction: Very bearish

Implied volatility: Low percentile and IV lower than SV

Protection: None

Intensity of investor monitoring: High; requires close monitoring

STRADDLES AND STRANGLES

The straddle (or the strangle) is a strategy that enables the trader to profit on movement regardless of the direction. Generally, the trader buys at-the-money puts and at-the-money calls with the same expiration. The strategy can be most effective when the options have a low percentile of IV at the time of entry. Once the position is entered, the trader can profit by a move of the stock price in either direction and/or an increase in implied volatility. Since the trader is buying both puts and calls at the same time, entry can be somewhat expensive and require a fair amount of capital. The risk is limited to the amount invested in buying the options (plus commissions), but the maximum risk occurs only if the positions are held to expiration and, at expiration, the stock price is exactly at the strike price of the options that were bought.

Reward is theoretically unlimited on the call side and limited on the put side only because a stock price cannot fall below zero.

Much the same can be said about strangles except that the trader purchases different strike price calls and puts. Since the calls and puts purchased are normally each out of the money, the premiums are less costly than they would be if purchased at the money as in the case of the straddle. However, since the options are at different strikes, the maximum risk (equal to the cost of entry) is spread over a wider range. If the price of the stock at option expiration falls anywhere between the strike price of the call and the strike price of the put, the maximum loss is realized.

Since the straddle and the strangle each involve buying time, I want to buy enough time to permit movement of the stock price and of volatility. I prefer to buy at least four months of time and often buy six months. One of the keys to successful straddle (or strangle) buying is to buy cheap, undervalued options on a stock where you expect movement. I look for IV in the lower percentiles where the IV is below the SV. Some subscription advisory services, such as Larry McMillan's *Option Strategist*, locate candidates that meet these criteria.

Synopsis of Straddles and Strangles

Relative risk: Limited

Capital required: Moderate to high

Potential reward: Unlimited

Time frame: Four months or longer

Expected market direction: Movement, not direction, is what is important

Implied volatility: Lower percentiles of IV and higher SV

Protection: None, but risk is limited to cost of entry

Intensity of investor monitoring: Moderate

BUYING STOCK

Almost every investor begins with or has experimented with the strategy of buying stock. Buying stock is highly capital intensive and is accompanied by high risk since the price theoretically could go to zero. Think about some of the former high flyers like Enron or WorldCom when you are tempted to pooh-pooh the idea that the great will not fall. Examples of huge drops are abundant; look at Cisco Systems (CSCO), which fell from a lofty $80 after eight splits to under $11 before starting a slow climb up. Make no mistake—buying stock without some form of protection, whether it is protective puts or stop loss orders, can be very risky business. However, the potential rewards are unlimited.

Historically, major markets have risen approximately two thirds of the time and dropped about one third of the time. That does not mean that all stocks move up when the market goes up, but many do. This phenomenon is, perhaps, the primary argument advanced by the buy-and-hold advocates because stocks do tend to go up in the long run. However, as the preeminent economist John Maynard Keynes once said: "In the long run we're all dead."

While an investor can reap great rewards from buying stock, I believe the high risks mandate that some protection be in place. Protective puts definitely limit the potential loss to the difference between the purchase price of the stock and the strike price of the put plus the premium paid for the put. These options do expire so the investor may be unwilling to regularly pay premiums to protect his investment.

Lesser protection is afforded by placing a stop loss or a trailing stop loss order. No stop loss order provides complete protection. If the stock gaps down on the morning open or after a halt in trading, for example, the stop would activate the sell order, but there is no guarantee at what price the order would be filled. At best, we know we could be out of the position, but unlike with the protective put, we would have no idea at what level.

A final modicum of protection might be found by using an alert. In theory, when the alert is received, we would close out position. The problem is that many investors will not respond to their own alerts. Instead of selling when the alert is received, they decide to let it go a few more pennies and then maybe a few more until the hole gets so deep that they then decide to wait until the price moves back up before selling. They have sprung the trap on themselves because they have failed to follow their own plan. Alerts simply do not work unless the trader has the absolute cold-blooded discipline to act. I would suggest that if you try alerts and find that you do not exit when one or two has been received, you should abandon them as a protective measure and at least place stops or trailing stops.

When we buy stock, our outlook is clearly bullish. There is no more bullish strategy except, perhaps, buying calls. The time frame of this strategy is indeterminate and is wholly dependent on the movement of the stock and your personal business plan.

Synopsis of Buying Stock

Relative risk: High without protection

Capital required: Large amount

Potential reward: Unlimited

Time frame: Indeterminate and depends on price movement and exit plan

Expected market direction: Bullish

Protection: None

Intensity of investor monitoring: Very high without adding protection

---

SELLING STOCK SHORT

In this strategy, we are trying to make money on a downward move of the stock price. We borrow the stock from our broker and sell it. Cash flows into our account at entry. At some point we will close the position by buying the stock to cover the position. While we are short the stock, we will be paying our broker interest on what we have borrowed.

This strategy has a potential reward that is limited only by the stock price's reaching zero. The maximum potential reward, then, is equal to the amount we receive from the sale of the borrowed stock less the commission paid. Risk is unlimited. If the stock takes off to the upside and we must buy to cover when the price has risen well above the price at which we sold, we could suffer a very significant loss or, theoretically at least, even be wiped out. While that concept may give rise to sobering thought, many traders have made a great deal of money—even fortunes—selling stock short. It is not a strategy to be ignored.

Since the risk, theoretically, is unlimited, serious thought should be given to having some protection in place. The highest level of protection would be to buy a protective call. If we owned the protective call and had to buy the stock to cover a short position, we could exercise our calls at the strike price we had chosen at any time until the options expired. The downside of the protective calls is that they expire and we must pay a premium to buy them. In order to profit overall, the stock price must fall enough by expiration to recoup the premium we paid for the calls plus commissions.

A second alternative to attempt to protect against large losses in the event a short sale turns against you (i.e., the stock price goes up) is to have a buy stop in place. That stop would initially be placed above your entry price so that when the stop was hit you would automatically buy to cover your short position. As with the case of a protective put, the price of the fill cannot be controlled and could be much different than desired in the event of a gap.

Setting an alert is a possible alternative, but the same dangers exist as explained in the last section; if you use an alert, you need to be disciplined enough to act on it.

As with buying a stock, the time in which you are short a stock is indeterminate. Many times, it seems a downward move happens quite quickly and you may be able to cover your short position profitably in a short span of time. Other times, it may take quite a while before an exit is reached. Keep in mind that you will be paying interest to your broker as long as you remain in the short position. Once again, your business plan will determine your exit strategy and the stock movement will determine when the exit will be reached.

Synopsis of Selling Stock Short

Relative risk: Very high without protection

Capital required: Opens with credit, and money is on hold; check with your broker

Potential reward: Maximum is amount received at time of short sale

Time frame: Indeterminate; depends on price movement and exit strategy

Expected market direction: Bearish

Protection: None

Intensity of investor monitoring: Very high without adding protection

---

WRITING COVERED CALLS

This strategy is one that is relatively capital intensive since the investor is buying stock. However, it is a little less costly than buying stock alone because we are also selling a call, which brings in a premium and reduces the net cost of the stock by the amount of premium received. Ignoring commissions for the moment, if we bought 1,000 shares of ABC at $15 a share, our cost would be $15,000. If we bought ABC at $15 and also sold 10 contracts of the $15 calls at $1.50 a share, our cost would be only $13,500 (pay $15,000 for the stock minus $1,500 received from the sale of the calls).

Writing covered calls is a bullish strategy because we own stock. We certainly do not want it to fall in price, so we should look for a neutral to bullish market for this strategy.

When writing covered calls, our reward is limited to the amount we receive from selling the calls plus the difference, if any, between the strike price we sold and the price we paid for the stock. In the preceding example, if we bought the stock for $15 a share and sold the at-the-money ($15) call for $1.50, the most we could make would be $1.50 a share less commissions. If the stock price were above $15 at expiration, we would be called out at $15, making no profit on the stock, but we would keep the $1.50 premium.

The risk in this strategy is similar to but less than the risk in just buying the stock. We have the risk that the stock price could fall to zero, but since the market pays us a premium to buy the calls, the risk is reduced by whatever we were paid for the calls.

When I am engaged in selling covered calls, I prefer to be called out of my position. I usually try to sell near-term (no more than five or six weeks on average) at-the-money calls. In that way, I am selling nothing but time value, and since time value dissipates faster and faster the closer the option gets to expiration, I often get a good bang for my buck. If, at expiration, the stock price is below the call strike I sold, I will reassess and either sell another near-term call or just exit the stock position.

Brokers may tell you that writing covered calls is not a particularly risky strategy, but be aware that the stock price could fall dramatically, even to zero. The strategy does provide a way to produce regular monthly income on long stock positions, and some investors who tend to have a long time frame may choose to sell out-of-the-money calls to generate income while attempting to retain their underlying position.

Synopsis of Writing Covered Calls

Relative risk: Similar to owning stock

Capital required: Fairly high, but somewhat less than just buying stock

Potential reward: Limited

Time frame: Depends on individual business plan

Market expectancy: Neutral to bullish

Implied volatility: Prefer to sell higher-percentile IV calls

Protection: None

Intensity of investor monitoring: Fairly high

SELLING NAKED PUTS

While a broker may tell you that writing covered calls is relatively safe, many may show alarm and tell you that selling naked puts is very risky.

The truth is that the risk of selling naked puts is equivalent to the risk of owning a stock and writing a covered call.

By selling a naked put we are undertaking the obligation to buy the stock at the strike price any time before expiration. In exchange for taking on the obligation, we are paid a premium. If the stock is assigned to us, our risk becomes the price we paid for the stock less the premium we received for selling the put.

Though the risk is the same as writing covered calls, the capital required when the trade is entered is significantly less, since money is flowing into our account at entry rather than out of it. Money is put on hold in our account to protect our broker, but entry into a naked put position results in a credit to our account. If the stock is assigned to us, there is then a significant capital requirement, since we are buying the stock. The capital requirement can be met, in some part, by the credit we received at the outset.

The reward is limited to the amount of premium collected less commission. Since this strategy involves the sale of an option, I almost always sell puts that are very close to expiration. In general, I like to sell puts that have a month or less remaining to expiration. In my own business plan, I sell only naked puts that are out-of-the-money and below some level of support. The strategy is definitely bullish, and the volatility picture is quite important.

Here, I am looking for a high percentile of IV, so I can sell options that are relatively expensive. I also want the percentile of IV to be greater than the percentile of SV so that the options are not only expensive but also overvalued.

Synopsis of Selling Naked Puts

Relative risk: Same as writing covered calls

Capital required: Credit on entry and money on hold in account; may have to buy stock

Potential reward: Limited to premium received

Time frame: Short

Market direction: Bullish

Implied volatility: High percentile

Protection: None

Intensity of investor monitoring: High

SELLING NAKED CALLS

Selling naked calls is the epitome of unlimited-risk, limited-reward trading. When employing this strategy, the trader receives a premium to undertake the obligation to sell stock he does not own at the strike price any time before expiration. The problem is that the trader would need to buy the stock to fulfill his obligation to sell at the strike price if he is "called." What an enormous risk that can be! The farm could literally be on the line. Suppose XYZ is trading at $19 a share and the trader sells the $20 calls and receives a $2-a-share premium. The company then becomes the target of competing takeover bids and the stock jumps $15 a share to $34. It is a certainty that the trader will be assigned at the $20 strike price, and he will have to buy the stock at $34 so he can fulfill his obligation to sell it at $20. The result would be an instant $14-a-share loss, which would be offset by the $2 premium initially received.

Theoretically, selling naked calls requires limitless capital and is so risky that a trader could be wiped out in a single trade. If a trader is using this dangerous strategy, I believe it should be on an extremely short time to expiration. Hours might be better than days, and the trader, even then, would have to evaluate whether the risk would be worth the probable small premium for so little time.

Since this strategy also involves a sale, one would look to sell expensive overvalued calls—a high percentile of IV and a lower percentile of SV.

Synopsis for Selling Naked Calls

Relative risk: Very high

Capital required: Credit on entry, but potentially enormous

Time frame: Very, very short

Expected market direction: Bearish

Protection: None (consider a spread instead)

Intensity of investor monitoring: Very high

BUYING ETFs, REITs, AND CLOSED-END FUNDS

Exchange-traded funds (ETFs), real estate investment trusts (REITs), and closed-end funds each trade like stocks, so what I said about buying stocks in this chapter applies to them with some distinctions that are worthy of note.

When we buy an ETF we are usually buying something that is broader than a single stock. We are buying something that tracks a market, sector, or at least some kettle of companies. Investment in ETFs removes at least some of the risk inherent in an individual stock. Our risk is still that the ETF could go to zero, but the likelihood of a whole market or a whole sector falling to nothing is much less likely than the risk of an individual stock's losing all or almost all of its value. A stock might crash because of something that happened with an officer of the company or because a competitor gains substantial market share, but such a happening would have a much lesser effect on the sector or market than on the individual stock.

As a result of a spread risk, ownership of market or sector ETFs involves a lesser practical risk than ownership of stock in individual companies. Much the same can be said of closed-end funds that own a variety of municipal bonds, for example. REITs also often own a variety of properties in a real estate sector and also spread some of the risk of ownership.

Since what we are buying is similar to a stock and trades like a stock, a fairly high amount of capital may be required to enter a position. The time frame is dependent on price movement and individual exit strategy. Positions in these investments should be monitored, but need not be watched quite as closely as positions in individual equities.

Synopsis for Buying ETFs, REITs, and Closed-End Funds

Relative risk: Less than individual stock ownership

Capital required: Relatively high

Potential reward: Unlimited

Time frame: Dependent on price movement and exit strategy

Expected market direction: Bullish

Protection: None

Intensity of investor monitoring: Moderate

SUMMARY

This final chapter is sort of a "cheat sheet" for comparing the strategies presented in this book. These comparisons give the reader a ready reference to the type of trade that fits his or her perception of market direction, trading budget, time frame, risk tolerance, and available time to monitor trades.

In Appendix D, we set out the comparison in a quick reference table to enable the investor to make a "down-and-dirty" search, after which he or she can return to the more detailed comparisons set out in this chapter or the in-depth treatment in the earlier chapters of this book.

I believe you now have a strong foundation. What is left is up to you. Good practice, good trading, and good luck.

Elements of a Basic Business Plan for Investors and Traders

The following is a quick checklist of elements you will want to consider in creating your personal business plan. I suggest that you answer each with great specificity. For example, for what strategies will I use, you would want to identify them specifically (e.g., buying calls or selling naked puts) rather than some overbroad statement (e.g., bullish strategies).

- ► Full time or part time?
- ► How much risk money will I assign?
- ► What are my business hours?
- ► What strategies will I use?
- ► When will I make trading decisions?
- ► What is the maximum number of trades at one time?
- ► What will trigger entry into a position?
- ► What will trigger my exit?
- ► What indicators will I use?
- ► What types of orders will I use?
- ► What are my expectations?

Closed-End Income-Producing Fund Examples

Following is an assortment of closed-end funds divided into categories of federal tax free, double tax free, insured, and taxable with high interest. The lists are not meant to be complete, since there are literally hundreds of funds in these categories. Neither are they recommendations; they are only a starting point for the investor's own investigation. It is critical that you make your own analysis before investing. It also is vital that you check the tax ramifications with your own tax professional before investing in any fund to determine the tax consequences at the time of your investment. The lists are definitely not exhaustive and are provided as examples only.

FEDERAL TAX FREE

APX: Blackrock Apex Municipal Fund

BBK: Blackrock Municipal Bond Trust

BFK: Blackrock Municipal Income Trust

BKK: Blackrock Muni 2020 Term Trust

BLE: Blackrock Municipal Income Trust II

DMF: Dreyfus Municipal Income Inc

DSM: Dreyfus Strat Muni Bond Fund

DTF: DTF Tax Free Inc Inc

EVN: Eaton Vance Municipal Income Trust

FMN: Federated Premier Muni Income Fund

FPT: Federated Premier Intermediate Muni Fund

IQI: Morgan Stanley Quality Municipal Income Trust

KSM: DWS Strategic Municipal Income Trust

KTF: DW Municipal Income Trust

LEO: Dreyfus Strategic Muni Inc

MFM: MFS Municipal Income Trust

MHD: Blackrock Muniholdings Fund Inc

MHF: Western Asset Municipal High Income Fund

MHI: Pioneer Muni High Income Trust

MNP: Western Asset Municipal Partners Fund Inc

MPT: Western Asset Municipal Partners Fund II Inc

MQT: Blackrock Muniyield Quality Fund II Inc

MQY: Blackrock Muniyield Quality Fund Inc

MVF: Blackrock Munivest Fund Inc

NIM: Nuveen Select Mat Muni Fund

NMA: Nuveen Muni Advantage Fund

NMI: Nuveen Muni Income Fund Inc

NMO: Nuveen Muni Market Opportunity Fund

NMZ: Nuveen Municipal High Income

NPF: Nuveen Premier Muni Income

NUV: Nuveen Muni Value Fund Inc

PMG: Putnam Municipal Bond Fund

VMQ: Van Kampen Municipal Trust

DOUBLE TAX FREE (FEDERAL AND STATE)

Arizona

VAZ: Delaware Investments Arizona Municipal Income Fund

California

AKP: Alliance California Municipal Income Fund

BFC: Blackrock CA Insured 08 Muni (also insured)

BFZ: Blackrock California Muni Income Trust

CEV: Eaton Vance California Municipal Income

EIA: Eaton Vance Insured California Muni Bond (also insured)

PZC: Pimco California Muni Income Fund III

Florida

BAF: Blackrock Florida Insured Muni Income Trust (also insured)

BRF: Blackrock Florida Insured Muni 2008 Term Trust (also insured)

EIF: Eaton Vance Insured FL Muni Bond Fund

FEV: Eaton Vance Florida Municipal Income Trust

MYF: Blackrock Muniyield Florida Fund

Georgia

NZX: Nuveen Georgia Dividend Advantage Muni Fund

Maryland

BZM: Blackrock Maryland Muni Bond Trust

Massachusetts

MAB: Eaton Vance Insured Mass Muni Bond Fund (also insured)

NMB: Nuveen Massachusetts Dividend Advantage

Michigan

EMI: Eaton Vance Municipal Income

MIW: Eaton Vance Insured Michigan Muni Bond (also insured)

New Jersey

BLJ: Blackrock NJ Muni Bond Trust

EMJ: Eaton Vance Insured NJ Muni Bond Fund (also insured)

New York

AYN: Alliance NY Muni Income Fund

BFY: Blackrock New York Muni Income Trust II

BQH: Blackrock NY Muni Bond Trust
ENX: Eaton Vance Insured NY Muni Bond Fund (also insured)
PMN: Putnam NY Inv Grade Muni Trust

Ohio

EIO: Eaton Vance Insured Ohio Muni Bond Fund (also insured)
EVO: Eaton Vance Ohio Municipal Income Trust

Pennsylvania

BPS: Blackrock Pennsylvania Strategic Municipal
EIP: Eaton Vance Insured Penns Muni Bond Fund (also insured)
EVP: Eaton Vance Pennsylvania Municipal Income Trust

INSURED

BYM: Blackrock Insured Muni Income Trust
EIA: Eaton Vance Insured California Muni Bond
EIO: Eaton Vance Insured Ohio Muni Bond Fund
EIP: Eaton Vance Insured Penns Muni Bond Fund
EIM: Eaton Vance Insured Municipal Bond Fund
EMJ: Eaton Vance Insured NJ Bond Fund
ENX: Eaton Vance Insured NY Muni Bond Fund
IIM: Morgan Stanley Insured Municipal Trust
IMB: Morgan Stanley Insured Municipal Bond Trust
IMS: Morgan Stanley Insured Muni Sec
IMT: Morgan Stanley Insured Muni Trust
MAB: Eaton Vance Insured Mass Muni Bond Fund
MIW: Eaton Vance Insured Michigan Muni Bond
MYI: Blackrock Muniyield Insured Fund Inc
NEA: Nuveen Insured Tax Free Advantage
NIF: Nuveen Premier Insured Muni
NIO: Nuveen Insured Muni Opportunity Fund

TAXABLE WITH HIGH INTEREST

EAD: Evergreen Income Advantage Fund

EFR: Eaton Vance Senior Floating Rate Trust

ERC: Evergreen Managed Inc Fund

ETB: Eaton Vance Tax-Managed Buy Write Income Fund

FCM: First Trust Four Corners

GHI: Global High Income Fund

GLU: Gabelli Global Utility and Income Trust

IGA: ING Global Advantage & Premium Opportunity Fund

IGD: ING Global Equity Dividend & Premium Opportunity Fund

JPG: Nuveen Equity Premium and Growth Fund

JPZ: Nuveen Equity Premium Income Fund

JSN: Nuveen Equity Premium Opportunity Fund

ZTR: Zweig Total Return Fund Inc

Selected ETFs and REITs

Following is a listing of the symbols and a brief explanation of various ETFs and REITs that are grouped by category and, as of the time of this writing, trade in a relatively liquid fashion. I have attempted to exclude ETFs that trade less than an average of 50,000 shares per day. The list is not meant to be comprehensive and is not a complete listing. It is offered as a starting point for further research on ETFs and REITs.

OVERALL MARKETS

DIA: Diamonds Trust ETF; tracks the Dow 30 Industrials.

IWM: iShares Russell 2000 Index; tracks the Russell 2000.

IWV: iShares Russell 3000 Index; tracks the Russell 3000.

QQQQ: Powershares QQQ Trust Series 1; tracks the Nasdaq 100.

SPY: Standard and Poor's Depository Receipts; tracks the S&P 500.

STYLES

IJR: iShares S&P Smallcap 600; tracks the Russell 600 small-cap stocks.

IWD: iShares Russell 1000 Value Index; tracks the Russell 1000 value stocks.

IWF: iShares Russell 1000 Growth Index; tracks the Russell 1000 growth stocks.

IWN: iShares Russell 2000 Value Index; tracks the Russell 2000 value stocks.

IWO: iShares Russell 2000 Growth Index; tracks the Russell 2000 growth stocks.

IWP: iShares Russell MidCap Growth Index; tracks the Russell midcap stocks.

IWW: iShares Russell 3000 Value Index; tracks the Russell 3000 value stocks.

IWZ: iShares Russell 3000 Growth Index; tracks the Russell 3000 growth stocks.

MDY: S&P SPDRS Depositary Receipts Midcap Trust Series; tracks S&P midcap stocks.

VV: Vanguard Large Cap; tracks large-cap stocks.

SECTORS

IAI: iShares U.S. Broker-Dealers Index; tracks the brokerage firms.

IBB: iShares Nasdaq Biotech Index; tracks biotech stocks.

IGE: iShares Goldman Sachs Natural Resources Index; tracks natural resources stock.

IGV: iShares Goldman Sachs Software Index; tracks software stocks.

XLB: SPDRS Select Sector Materials; tracks stocks in the basic materials sector.

XLE: SPDRS Select Sector Energy; tracks stocks in the energy sector.

XLF: SPDRS Select Sector Financial; tracks stocks in the financial sector.

XLI: SPDRS Select Sector Industrial; tracks stocks in the industrial sector.

XLK: SPDRS Select Sector Technology; tracks stocks in the tech sector.

XLP: SPDRS Select Sector Consumer Staples; tracks in the consumer staples sector.

XLU: SPDRS Select Sector Utilities; tracks stocks in the utilities sector.

XLV: SPDRS Select Sector Health Care; tracks health care stocks sector.

XLY: SPDRS Select Sector Consumer Discretionary; tracks stocks in the discretionary sector.

FOREIGN EQUITIES

The following are all iShares MSCI Index Funds for the countries listed:

EWA: Australia

EWC: Canada

EWD: Sweden

EWG: Germany

EWH: Hong Kong

EWI: Italy

EWJ: Japan

EWK: Belgium

EWL: Switzerland

EWM: Malaysia

EWN: Netherlands

EWO: Austria

EWP: Spain

EWQ: France

EWS: Singapore

EWT: Taiwan

EWU: United Kingdom

EWW: Mexico

REITs (REAL ESTATE INVESTMENT TRUSTS) BY CATEGORY

Health Care

HCN: Healthcare REIT Inc.

HR: Healthcare Realty Trust

LTC: LTC Properties

NHP: Nationwide Health Properties

SNH: Seniorhousing Properties Trust

Hotel/Motel

BEE: Strategic Hotels & Resorts, Inc.

DRH: Diamondrock Hospitality

ENN: Equity Inns, Inc.
FCH: Felcor Lodging Trust
HST: Host Hotels & Resorts, Inc.
KPA: Innkeepers USA Trust
SPPR: Supertel Hospitality, Inc.

Office

ARE: Alexandria Real Estate Equities
BDN: Brandywine Real Estate Trust
BXP: Boston Properties
LRY: Liberty Property Trust
OFC: Corporate Office Properties Trust

Residential

AIV: Apartment Investment & Mortgage Company
ARC: Affordable Residential Communities, Inc.
ASN: Archstone Smith Trust
AVB: Avalonbay Communities
EQR: Equity Residential
FICC: Fieldstone Investment Corp.
HME: Home Properties, Inc.
PPS: Post Properties, Inc.
UDR: UDR, Inc.

Retail

CBL: CBL & Associates Properties
EQY: Equity One, Inc.
GGP: General Growth Properties, Inc.
KIM: Kimco Realty Corp.
NNN: National Retail Properties, Inc.
O: Realty Income Corp.
SKT: Tanger Factory Outlet
TCO: Taubman Centers, Inc.

Strategy Comparison

This table sets out various strategies for easy comparison of the relative potential risk and reward levels, the initial capital that might be required, the length of time one might expect to be in the position, what protection may be available, how much time is required "baby-sitting" the trade, and the market direction you want to see if you are using the particular strategy.

TABLE D.1 Comparison of Strategies

Strategy	Risk	Reward	Initial Capital Required	Time Frame	Protection	Level of Monitoring Required	Market Direction
Collar	Zero to limited	Limited	High	+/- One year	Built in	Very low	Bullish
Buy stock with protective put	Limited	Unlimited	High	Depends on put expiration	Built in	Moderate	Bullish
Short stock with protective call	Limited	Limited only by stock going to zero	Credit on entry	Depends on call expiration	Built in	Moderate	Bearish
Bullish put spread	Limited	Limited	Credit on entry	Short: Six weeks or less	Built in	Moderate to high	Neutral to bullish
Bearish call spread	Limited	Limited	Credit on entry	Short: Six weeks or less	Built in	Moderate to high	Neutral to bearish
Iron condor	Limited	Limited	Credit on entry	Short: Six weeks or less	Built in	Moderate to high	Neutral
Bullish call spread	Limited	Limited	Low to moderate	Four months or greater	Built in	Moderate	Bullish
Bearish put spread	Limited	Limited	Low to moderate	Four months or greater	Built in	Moderate	Bearish
Buying calls	Limited	Unlimited	Low to moderate	At least four months	None	High	Bullish

Strategy							
Buying puts	Limited	Unlimited to stock price zero	Low to moderate	Four to six months	None	High	Bearish
Straddles/Strangles	Limited	Unlimited	Moderate	About six months	Built in	Moderate	Movement in either direction
Buying stock	Only limited by entry price	Unlimited	High	Depends on price and exit strategy	None	High	Bullish
Selling stock short	Unlimited	Limited	Credit on entry	Depends on price and exit strategy	None	Very high	Bearish
Writing covered calls	Limited only by entry price	Limited	High	Short, but can be long if "buy-and-hold" investor	None	Moderate to high	Bullish
Selling naked Puts	Limited by stock price going to zero	Limited	Credit on entry	Short: One month or less	None	High	Bullish

Recommended Reading

S o much has been written over the years about stock and option trading that little is truly new. Many of the subjects I have covered have been treated by other authors as well though not necessarily in the same way. The following is a list of publications that have been extremely helpful to me in my trading education and career. I want to credit the authors and the content of their books for much of my knowledge and the ultimate creation of this book.

Achelis, Steven, *Technical Analysis from A to Z* (New York: McGraw-Hill, 1995)

Block, Ralph L., *The Essential REIT* (San Francisco: Brunston Press, 1997)

Elder, Alexander, *Trading for a Living* (New York: John Wiley & Sons, 1993)

Elder, Alexander, *Come into My Trading Room* (New York: John Wiley & Sons, 2002)

Hagstrom, Robert, *The Essential Buffett* (New York: John Wiley & Sons, 2001)

Kiyosaki, Robert, and Sharon Lechter, *Rich Dad, Poor Dad* (New York: Warner Books, 2000)

Lefevre, Edwin, *Reminiscences of a Stock Operator* (New York: George H. Doran Company, 1923)

Lehman, Richard, and Lawrence G. McMillan, *New Insights on Covered Call Writing* (Princeton: Bloomberg Press, 2003)

McMillan, Lawrence G., *Options as a Strategic Investment*, 4th edition (New York: New York Institute of Finance, 2002)

McMillan, Lawrence G., *Profit with Options* (New York: John Wiley & Sons, 2002)

Natenberg, Sheldon, *Option Volatility and Pricing* (New York: McGraw-Hill, 1994)

Nelson, Miles, and Darlene Nelson, *Stock Split Secrets* (Seattle: Lighthouse, 2000)

Nison, Steve, *Japanese Candlestick Charting Techniques* (New York: New York Institute of Finance, 1991)

Nison, Steve, *The Candlestick Course* (Hoboken, NJ: John Wiley & Sons, 2003)

Options Clearing Corporation, *Characteristics and Risks of Standardized Options* (pamphlet) (Chicago: Author, 1987)

Sutton, Doug, *Beginning Investors Bible* (Seattle: Lighthouse, 2001)

Yates, Leonard, *High Performance Options Trading* (Hoboken, NJ: John Wiley & Sons, 2003)

Index